"Webinars are the fastest growing form of corporate learning event, yet they are often boring, too long, and invite multi- or even triple-tasking. *The Webinar Manifesto* is an important and brave look at redesigning and refocusing our online connected learning time."

—**Elliott Masie**
Chair, The Learning CONSORTIUM

"Whether you are running webinars for sales, marketing, or e-learning, your ability to create rich and engaging experiences for your audience directly impacts the ROI of your event. *The Webinar Manifesto* provides a set of principles and tools that will help you transform flat and boring webinars into rich and engaging experiences."

—**Guillaume Privat**
Director, Adobe Connect

"*The Webinar Manifesto* is a wake-up call to action for anyone who delivers live online learning. The book's witty and fun format gives frank advice and practical tips through its seven design-and-delivery principles. The authors have declared war on bad webinars and invite you to join them. I've signed the Webinar Manifesto. You should too!"

—**Cindy Huggett**
Author, Virtual Training Basics

D0367383

"The Webinar Manifesto is an inspirational book, with easy-to-follow principles and practical tips that will help you create and develop next-generation killer webinars. I highly encourage you to join the movement and declare war on bad webinars!"

—**Christopher Pappas**
Founder of the eLearningIndustry.com and the
Instructional Design and eLearning Professionals' Group

"Like any legitimate manifesto, this book hits the mark by causing you to think and challenge the status quo. Building on the underlying angst of the zealot's cause, this book provides a practical, smart, and real-world guide to immediately improving your webinar experience. Matt and Treion are spot on."

—**Frank Rogers**
President/CEO InteSolv

THE WEBINAR MANIFESTO

TREION
MULLER

MATTHEW
MURDOCH

THE REVOLUTION BEGINS WITH YOU.

 STEP 1 READ THE BOOK. If it lights you up, if it connects with your experience and your passion for something better, then go to…

TheWebinarManifesto.com

 STEP 2 And SIGN THE MANIFESTO. Once you've SIGNED the MANIFESTO, then…

 STEP 3 Begin the battle and SHARE THE MANIFESTO with others.

STEP 4 SHARE YOUR SUCCESSES with the community.

not EVER

present, teach,
facilitate, instruct,
inform, or ENGAGE

NEVER DESIGN, DELIVER, OR SELL

market, advertise,
PITCH, plug, or push

instructional,
GRAPHICAL, platform,
or cosmetic

crappy, PATHETIC, poor,
bad, awful, BORING,
stupid, or WASTEFUL

ABSOLUTELY
not ever!

LOUSY WEBINARS AGAIN

virtual classroom,
WEBCAST, online seminar,
or any SYNCHRONOUS
web conference live-online
training session

ISBN 978-1-936111-33-6

Printed in the United States of America.

TABLE OF CONTENTS

MEET THE ENEMY

DECLARATION OF WAR

We're declaring war—on bad webinars.

And we want you to join us.

This is a revolution and, like most revolutions, this one is both

2

AGAINST SOMETHING

and

FOR SOMETHING.

WHAT WE ARE FIGHTING AGAINST:

We're against Zombie webinars where the walking dead hang out in cyberspace, begging for someone to put them out of their digital misery.

We're against mundane, talking-head PowerPoint® presentations.

We're against insanity—doing webinars the same way we always do, even when they keep failing.

We're against working in silos.

We're against vapor-world experiences—where no one talks, no one interacts, no one shares—it's just me, my webinar, and—nothing...

...VAPOR.

3

We've tolerated and nurtured the webinar as it is for years. We've made some real advances and done some very cool things. We're closer than ever to getting past the machine and up next to the people. But we still have a long way to go. And we don't believe that webinars can continue to evolve incrementally, like some single-celled amoeba waiting another million years to get closer to the edge of the ooze and start growing some legs. We must speed up the evolutionary process. This needs to be more caterpillar/butterfly and less dinosaur/human.

And so we're declaring war on bad webinars, and we want you to join us. We want you to join us in committing to KEEP doing the things that work and STOP doing the things that don't work, that never worked...

...THAT WILL NEVER WORK.

WHAT WE ARE FIGHTING FOR:

We're for captivating audiences through eloquent delivery and beautiful design.

We're for pushing the limits of our technology.

We're for amplifying what works and eliminating what doesn't.

We're for synergy and sharing.

We're for better transformational webinar design and delivery. In our previous book, *The Learning eXPLOSION*, we laid out some of the rules we should follow to create great webinars. Now we're taking those rules to the street—to you.

4

THIS REQUIRES ACTION.

And that action comes out of 7 MANIFESTO PRINCIPLES...

...FOUR PRINCIPLES focus on NEXT-GENERATION DESIGN while

...THREE PRINCIPLES focus on NEXT-GENERATION DELIVERY.

WHY DOES IT MATTER?

Becoming proficient on webinar platforms is no longer an option, it is a requisite in today's global marketplace. When listing your skills on your LinkedIn profile or résumé, "webinar delivery" would be a timely and an extremely beneficial skill to add, whether you are in sales, training, marketing, or leadership management.

For example, with webinars...

- Trainers can facilitate sessions to their distributed workforces.

- Leaders can launch initiatives internationally.

- Marketers can reach their channels more easily and more cost-efficiently.

- You can work from home (in your pajamas if you like).

- More time is spent in the office instead of on the road.

- Travel costs are decreased and you can contribute to the "green" movement.

- You can also protect against age discrimination. If you don't use a webcam, no one can see how old or young you are.

5

WHAT ARE WE FIGHTING? MEET THE "WEBBENYS."

As in any battle, the ideas brewing around the campfires of the revolutionaries and sparking the fires that burn in the hearts of those manning the barricades need a reason to be. (Do you like that Les Mis moment?) Who needs a Webinar Manifesto if webinars work just fine as they are? Who's going to join a campaign against something that's working? But webinars aren't working—at least a large chunk of the time.

WILL YOU JOIN US? If you believe as we do—webinars aren't working as they should, platforms are as limiting as they are engaging, meetings are too often boring, and the engagement of bright minds is too often limited or missing completely—then join us.

Each element of this manifesto is a response to something that isn't working in the webinar world. Maybe we've fallen into a "platform habit" where we fail to challenge or stretch the limits of the platform and fail to try to present in new and bolder ways. Maybe we've sacrificed engagement for PowerPoint slides that are easy to create, easy to present, but painful to endure. Whatever the failure—whether we've done something too often or too little; whether we've forgotten people accidentally or intentionally—there are real problems in our webinar world.

Those problems are the enemy. Defeating each problem, overcoming each limitation, and revisiting each system or structure are key to winning this battle. This manifesto was formed to combat this list of enemies. The purpose of each principle in the manifesto is to inspire each of us to stop doing something average and start doing something great!

6

To help us remember what we're stopping—the enemies at the gates so to speak—we've given them a name:

WEBBENY.

The Webinar Manifesto is a declaration of the principles that will inspire and sustain our war against the Webbeny— the webinar enemy.

We invite you to identify and share your own Webbeny list on your favorite network, and explain how you defeated or destroyed them. So to use the language of another great battle: "Will you join in our crusade? Will you be strong and stand with [us]—on the barricades?"

CONNECT OR DIE

TWITTER SUMMARY

If you do it alone, you'll crash. Connect 2 others with your digital umbilicus, jump into the virtual abyss, & continue 2 lengthen the cord.

Think extreme sports. What comes to mind?

Do words like DANGEROUS,

DARING,

INSANE,

and RISKY work?

To manage the risk, some of these sports require you to be connected to a lifesaving device.

Most mountain climbers don't free-climb or "solo"—climbing without ropes. Some people free-dive without an oxygen supply, but most divers, even extreme divers, carry a source of breathable gases. If you jump off a bridge, you'll most likely be attached to a rubber band.

One of the earliest and most extreme examples of an extreme sport wasn't actually a sport, wasn't necessarily defined as "extreme," and didn't even happen on this planet. On March 18, 1965, Alexei Leonov and Pavel Belyayev hurled into space aboard *Voskhod 2*, a two-seat rocket. Ninety minutes into the twenty-six hour flight, Leonov opened the outer hatch and pushed himself out to the end of his 17-foot umbilicus— becoming the first man to walk in space.

10

11

Experience the first space walk:
http://youtu.be/5xjaYSLWYOc

Spacewalking, like other extreme activities, requires a connection to survive (at least if you want to do them twice).

Webinars can also be extreme, if you choose to push the limits (which we're encouraging throughout this book). In order to do this and break free from the mundane—and survive— you need to be connected to a relevant network of people and organizations who can both push you to try the "extreme" and help you survive your webinar.

All alone with your problems, your challenges, your deadlines, and the brain freeze that can invade any webinar, you just might feel like you're experiencing the slow, painful death of "I don't know what to do; I'm never going to get this; I'm going to miss my deadline; my head will be on a platter."

Take a deep breath!

DON'T CRASH!

CONNECT...

Connecting allows you to find NEW SOLUTIONS, INSIGHTS, and gain access to experts who can help you SURVIVE and THRIVE.

Engage and re-engage and work on a solution together. Because today you're out on the edge, tomorrow will be our turn, and you're going to be as important to us then as we are going to be to you today. In rock climbing, at one moment you're leading the ascent, and the next you're "belaying" or protecting the person now taking the lead. In webinars, one day you're at the end of the tether, the next you're anchoring it for someone else.

This manifesto principle is about connecting outside your traditional circle of friends and fellow employees. It's not about having a lifeline DURING the webinar; it's about connecting with people with similar interests and expertise BEFORE and AFTER the webinar.

> ### MEET THE WEBBENY:
> The Webbeny is doing it alone—not connecting to webinar communities, resources, and experts.

THE WEBINAR UMBILICUS

As webinar designers and deliverers, we all have days when we can't conceive it, plan it, organize it, create it, deliver it, just plain do it on our own. That's the time to reach for the cord. Throw out your lifeline and see who will grab on to help!

COME ON! We need to get over the notion that we're all competing against each other.

Let's share what we've learned and learn from what others have shared. The webinar experience ties us all together; the webinar umbilicus connects us and is the springboard to new opportunities...

...IF WE'LL ALL GRAB ON.

1. ATTACH THE CORD

Commit yourself, today, to never doing ANYTHING on your own again. Don't try to think through it alone, work through it alone, solve it, suggest it, summarize it, or share it —alone. You have the resources, unlike any other time in history, to engage the best minds around YOUR issue. You may collect and reject a lot of what you're offered, but that's a lot better than winging it all on your own. There are experts out there— find them, meet with them, listen to them, use them.

13

ATTACH YOUR CORD TO SOCIAL MEDIA
There are over 2.8 billion social-media profiles representing around half of all Internet users worldwide.

f   1 billion active users

🐦   500+ million accounts   } As of 2012

in 150+ million users

You Tube   One hour of video is uploaded to YouTube every second. (You do the math...that's a lot of video.)

To get an idea of how social media is growing, check out "Social Media Count" (http://www.personalizemedia.com/the-count/)

CONNECTION ACTION: Find resources that can connect you to others. These might be professional sites like LinkedIn or social sites like Facebook. They might be general-interest gathering places or very task- or job-specific chat rooms where experts gather to share specific problems and synergize solutions. Try connecting with some of these groups and people:

- eMarketing Association Network
- The eLearning Guild
- ASTD
- Cindy Huggett (cindyhuggett.com)
- Wayne Turmel (greatwebmeetings.com)
- David Smith (insynctraining.com)
- Christopher Pappas (elearningindustry.com)
- Becky Pluth (bobpikegroup.com)
- Roger Courville (TheVirtualPresenter.com)
- Connect with us on Twitter (@learningexplosn), on Facebook, and on LinkedIn. We love to collaborate with members of the movement.

If you don't know where to start, it's the 21st century, for heaven's sake… Google it!

A bit of caution. At the end of Leonov's 12-minute spacewalk, his dream turned into a nightmare. His spacesuit had inflated in the vacuum of space, making movement difficult and reentry through the door of the spaceship impossible. He was eventually able to open a valve to bleed off some of the suit's pressure and was barely able to squeeze inside the capsule. Protect yourself against "overinflating." Don't inflate your network with unnecessary people or too many options. This will take some practice—most of it the "school of hard knocks" kind—but learn to be wise and connect to the smallest group of people and the tightest circle of ideas that will meet your needs.

2. JUMP

Open the hatch and take your first step into the social-media abyss. You'll soon find that there's a lifeline that will support you. Once you get out of your cubicle and start building networks of people who are both able and willing to help, engage them constantly. Send them questions, text them challenges, tweet for help. Make every solution an "us" solution. Your social connections allow you to get next to people and begin the critical, synergistic conversations that can lead to world-changing solutions. Don't just chat with people. Don't just "like" something—engage with it, learn it, turn it, twist it around, and wring out a new and unique idea from that engagement.

15

> **CONNECTION ACTION:** Pay attention to what others have to offer. Technologies like tweeting and texting are rapid-fire ways to get "in the moment" insight. Take those tweets and texts, and gather them together. On numerous occasions, we've thrown a lifeline request out to LinkedIn groups. Within minutes, we typically have received great solutions and innovative thinking to solve our problems.

3. LENGTHEN THE CORD

Make what you learn available, not only to the folks on your webinar umbilicus, but to the world at large. Become part of the synergistic sharing that is the Web. Who knows, you might stumble onto people who want to join your network and bring with them not only their own ideas and insights, but a whole gang you never knew existed. When we post what we've learned, what we've created, what our synergy has produced, we not only lift the whole game, but we announce our presence to all gamers. We declare that we've arrived, that we're thinking, and that we're looking for people to think, solve, and work with us. And the cord just gets longer.

> **CONNECTION ACTION:** Throughout this book, we will provide you space to jot down thoughts and to practice the Lengthen the Cord principle called the "Manifesto Chronicles." Remember, we're all in this together, and your thoughts and solutions must be shared with others.

MANIFESTO CHRONICLES

Ideas, solutions, and other cool resources

THE LAST WORD

Don't try and go it alone. Find ideas, best practices, and creative solutions for your webinars by connecting with like-minded individuals before and after your webinar. Get out of your cubicle, get out of your silo, get out of the groupthink that surrounds. Reach out, grab onto the electrons that form the virtual cord—and once you are attached, jump. Find some friends who will think with you, solve with you, and share with you. Then make sure you lengthen the cord yourself by sharing what you learn with others.

DON'T DIE ALONE...
CONNECT!

There's a whole world out there just waiting to grab on if they know you're falling.

17

PUTTING PRINCIPLE TO PRACTICE (KEY SUMMARY POINTS)

To survive the constant evolution of webinar platforms and influx of new studies and information regarding webinar best practices, it is essential that you tap into the online network of relevant thought leaders and communities.

THREE "CONNECT OR DIE" ACTIONS:

1. Attach the Cord. Never do anything alone. Get connected to relevant networks of people and organizations. Let's build this industry together.

2. Jump. If you haven't done so already, be an active participant in relevant social-media and networking sites. Seek advice, synergy, and help, but don't inflate your connections with too many people or too many networks.

3. Lengthen the Cord. Share what you learn with your connections and networks. Contribute to the community.

DON'T DEFAULT

🐦 TWITTER SUMMARY

Webinar platforms come with default settings. Learn what they are, try them, move beyond them, then throw away the manual & author your own.

Have you ever seen or, better still, been part of a group that decides to jump off a cliff at the local swimming hole? There are at least two interesting things to watch. One is approach, the other is execution. We don't know how the physics work but, for some reason, things always look higher when you're looking down from them than when you're looking up at them. What seemed like no big deal at the water's edge is a whole different story when you're standing on the cliff looking down at the water. This difference in perspective—coupled with experience and skill—affects how each prospective diver approaches the edge. Some are confident, some are cautious, and some are hell-bent on just lettin' 'er rip.

Whether uncomfortable, cautious, or ready to go, once fear is contained, it is time to execute...

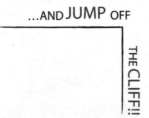

...AND JUMP OFF

THE CLIFF!!

And this is where it can get really interesting. Some jump, some dive, some get fancy. Some come off graceful and experienced, others awkward and obviously new at it. Some seem to have a plan they can't quite execute, while others roll, tuck, and arch in near perfect form.

While individuals have their own experiences and perceptions about both approach and execution,

THERE IS ONE THING THAT ALL SHARE IN COMMON—THE PLATFORM.

Whether you're new at it or it's old hat for you, you're jumping off the same cliff. Whether you've got a plan or are just hoping to survive, everyone jumps off the same cliff. Whether you come off elegant or awkward, everyone jumps off the same cliff—the same platform.

A webinar platform is just that—a platform. It offers the same launching pad for the inexperienced and the expert. It provides a place to try something new (and maybe a little bit scary) or something you've done a thousand times before. The platform itself is not what shapes either approach or execution. That is the province of people on the platform and what they will do with their launch pad.

DON'T DEFAULT AND ABANDON CONTROL AND CREATIVITY TO THE PLATFORM.

Don't let your approach, your plan, or your execution be controlled solely by the platform you choose. It's a jumping-off point or a beginning, nothing more. Your job is to shape the platform to your ends. It's the place you start from. It's the jumping-off point.

MEET THE WEBBENY:
Every webinar platform comes with default bare-bones settings. Left as they are, without any modifications, they become the Webbeny.

CREATING THE JUMPING-OFF POINT

One of the reasons some jumpers execute so well while others flail wildly is that the more elegant often have more experience and know what can and can't be done from the platform (the cliff edge) they've chosen. The webinar platform you choose has far more potential than is usually tapped, but only if you understand how to shape the platform to your ends rather than being contained by it.

There are four steps you can take with any webinar platform that will activate the second principle—Don't Default.

1. Awareness: Read the Manual

2. Attempt: Try the Manual

3. Assimilate: Apply the Manual

4. Author: Write Your Own Manual

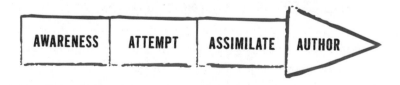

1. AWARENESS: READ THE MANUAL

Stefano Marzano, former CEO and Chief Creative Director, Philips Design, has a passion for next-generation approaches to technology and technology-based products. In an article titled "Finding Your Sculpture" (November 27, 2007), he describes a concept called "Sense and Simplicity." Introduced in 2004, this concept outlines an approach to create products that are meaningful (make sense) and accessible (simple).

Wouldn't it be nice if everyone, including platform designers, thought that way?

There's still work to be done to figure out and then offer a platform that is `sensible`—does the things most of us want and doesn't do the things we care little or nothing about. Most of us would also like our platform to be `simple`—accessible and intuitive—and obvious in connecting what we want to do with what the platform can do.

Until we get to that point, we'll still rely, at least to some extent, on "the manual." It may be a virtual manual, a series of videos on YouTube, or a PDF that no longer requires the slaughter of trees to create, but it's still a manual. And unless you've already mastered a given platform, this is where you start.

But unfortunately, manuals typically suck. These humongous bricks (or files) have small fonts, are extremely boring, and are packed with far too many words and not nearly enough pictures.

An example of a company that gets the concept of simple and intuitive instructions is IKEA, the Swedish furniture mega-box store. With their simple illustrations and NO written instructions, they seem capable of producing instructions easy enough to build a nuclear power plant. There are a lot of webinar-platform providers who could learn from IKEA's simplicity approach to the act of writing manuals.

We know almost nobody starts with the manual, but a detailed awareness of what the platform offers is...

...THE STARTING POINT.

Once you know what it CAN do, you can start worrying about getting that platform to do what you WANT it to do. Skip this step and you'll likely experience one of the following:

THIS @#$%&! THING DOESN'T WORK—

you can't get the platform to do what you need it to do.

HOW MANY @#$%&! BUTTONS ARE THERE?—

you may be able to get started, but you get lost and confused very quickly.

THAT'S AMAZING! NOW WHAT THE @#$%&! DID I JUST DO?—

you have no idea what you just did or how to do it again.

So unless you want to start lost or get lost, read the manual—in fact, STUDY the manual, at least once.

Most of the platform providers have their manuals or resource centers available online.

LEADING WEBINAR-PLATFORM RESOURCE SITES

JUST GOOGLE...

- Adobe Connect User Manual
- WebEx User Manual
- GoToWebinar User Manual
- Live Meeting User Manual
- Saba Centra User Manual
- ReadyTalk User Manual
- iLinc User Manual
- IBM Sametime User Manual
- Blackboard Collaborate User Manual

2. ATTEMPT: TRY THE MANUAL

Now that you've got a reasonable familiarity with the basics of what the platform can do, put it through its paces. Design a webinar, but stick to the fundamentals—don't get fancy yet.

The goal here is to land

ALIVE,

not to land

PRETTY.

No jackknifes, tucks, somersaults, or rolls—just a clean, safe jump into unknown waters.

It may be helpful, in these early stages, to document what you're doing or trying. Maybe go old school and keep some basic notes scrawled out in a binder or record yourself doing 10 to 15 webinars. It is a great way to test the technology as well as to see how you come across as a virtual presenter. It's something that is really hard to do in the physical world where you would need a camera crew, but it's very easy to do in a virtual world.

What you're looking for at this phase is a clean presentation, designed to deliver a message and stimulate an engaging conversation. Create a presentation that is simple to deliver—not too complex or too technically convoluted. Just get off the cliff and into the water.

Try a few presentations at this level, maybe as many as a half dozen before you move to the next step.

3. ASSIMILATE: APPLY THE MANUAL

This is where we begin to break away from the simple default options of the platform. This is where we start to get fancy and, more importantly, where we start to make the platform our own. We make it our own when we get the platform to work WITH us and FOR our audience. It's where we separate and prioritize what we've learned in the first steps into what we'll keep and use and what we'll ignore or discard. It's where we practice, fail, and practice some more until we get it right.

Since we've made the (sometimes) painful commitment to become fundamentally "aware" of the platform as designed, and since we've now practiced with that design in the "Attempt" phase, we've garnered enough intelligence—through both assimilation of the information and application in real-world presentations—to start making decisions.

We assimilate, not by taking the platform at face value, but in a process requiring two decisions:

1. **KEEP AND USE–** Which features and functions of the platform work for both my audience and me? Which of those features will I put at the top of my webinar toolbox? What will become my "A," "B," and "C" priorities in this platform? Making these decisions will drive you to spend more time on high-priority features, thus increasing your skill, your elegance, and your outcomes.

EXAMPLE: Our top tools are chat, polling, PowerPoint presentations, and prerecorded video (not webcam).

2. IGNORE AND DISCARD– Some features might be okay in some situations but not in most. Put these in the "ignore" pile. You'll pay little attention to these in most design-and-delivery scenarios, but you'll know they're there if you ever decide to go back to them. Discard features (not necessarily from the platform software but from the "software" between your own ears) that don't work for you. Something that appears helpful and elegant to one person may be seen as confusing and awkward to someone else. It's as important to decide what you'll ignore in the platform as what you'll use.

EXAMPLE: We typically don't use a lot of whiteboarding, even though it's available on our platforms. The additional whiteboard buttons and tools take valuable time to maneuver and occasionally cause more distraction than interaction. So we've found other ways of getting people engaged in our webinars without whiteboards.

4. AUTHOR: WRITE YOUR OWN MANUAL

Now,

THROW AWAY THE MANUAL

and never (or at least, hardly ever) look at it again.

It's time to experiment with new jumps and tricks and to author your own handbook. This is the most important method to avoid defaulting back to the same old way of doing things.

In the "Assimilate" phase, you sort and decide—you pick out the pieces and features of the platform that will work best for you. But you're picking, sorting, and deciding on what you've learned from the platform. Now you're finally ready to innovate, you're ready to author a manual—including those features you like and rejecting those you don't.

You should probably author your own manual for every platform you use. But to get to this point, it's critical that, if necessary, you force yourself to go through all the preceding steps. If you don't take the time to build awareness of what the platform offers, it's hard to make a real attempt at making that platform work successfully. And without some experience under your belt with the platform "as is," you can't decide what to assimilate and what to reject. Finally, it's that list of assimilate/keep and eliminate/reject items that becomes the content of your own personalized "manual" for a given platform.

If you want to stop defaulting and start using webinar platforms as a beginning rather than an end—literally a jumping-off point—then you're going to have to work the process, pay the price, and develop the skill to do more than just hit the water and not die.

When we started writing our own manual, we began with one main question: "What is best for the learner?" When you start with this question rather than, "What limitations does my platform have?" you start to see new solutions, where before there were none.

31

For example, once we were conducting a webinar for a company in which there were going to be three groups in different conference rooms listening in. Since not everyone was going to have their own computer, we couldn't use the polling feature or even the chat feature the way they were intended. Instead, we conducted an "offline" activity. Assuming nearly everyone had a smartphone, we asked questions and had them search online for the answer. They shouted out the answers when they found them. It got everyone engaged, and we added a new chapter to our own manual.

THE LAST WORD

Conducting a webinar is as different from live in-person training or a face-to-face meeting as jumping off a cliff is to jumping off your bed. You mustn't default to traditional approaches. Good-quality online events must be designed and delivered much differently.

Just throwing what you usually use on the platform can be a bad idea…

IT'S A DIFFERENT APPROACH…

A DIFFERENT JUMPING-OFF SPOT…

DIFFERENT HEIGHT…

DIFFERENT OPPORTUNITIES.

You could fall flat on your face if you do it how you have always done it…

SO DON'T DEFAULT.

32

PUTTING PRINCIPLE TO PRACTICE (KEY SUMMARY POINTS)

With the continual upgrades to existing platforms and the constant development of new ones, it's also imperative to stay alert and be aware of new and better possibilities. You may have to walk through the four A's a few more times with different platforms to find the one that best fits your needs.

FOUR STEPS TO NOT DEFAULT:

1. Awareness. Read the manual. Actually study it. Learn everything your platform can and cannot do.
2. Attempt. Try the manual. Try some things in your webinar platform, but don't get fancy yet.
3. Assimilate. Apply the manual. Begin to break away from the default options of the platform and make it your own. It's in this step that you choose what you should keep and use, and ignore and discard.
4. Author. Write your own manual. Experiment with new jumps and tricks. Ask yourself what is best for the learner and then proceed respectively.

Beyond the platform, there are at least four other areas where you should NOT DEFAULT:

- How you market and advertise your webinar.
- Using PowerPoint and other presentation tools.
- Building the handouts for your webinar experience.
- Delivering the webinar experience.

You will find the principles needed to refrain from defaulting in these areas in Principle 3—Shut Down the Ugly.

Ideas, solutions, and other cool resources

MANIFESTO CHRONICLES

Ideas, solutions, and other cool resources

SHUT DOWN THE UGLY

SHUT DOWN THE UGLY

TWITTER SUMMARY

Beautify all aspects of your webinar: email, presentations, handouts, social media, marketing, & the webinar experience.

Taking what was once boring and ugly, and magically transforming it into a piece of art, is not only a real skill but something of real value. Fortunately, ugly is being shut down all around us.

Not only in the art world but in the business world, you'll see the brush strokes of the marketer, the advertiser, and the graphic artist, each charged with the exhilarating responsibility of shutting down the ugly while transforming the ugly duckling of the moment into a beautiful swan.

38

As an example of transforming the mundane into the magnificent, take any popular carbonated soda. Soda is simply carbonated water, sugar (sucrose or high-fructose corn syrup), sometimes caffeine, phosphoric acid, colorants (depending on the intended color of the drink), and a minuscule amount of natural flavorings. There's nothing special or beautiful about the basic ingredients. That's where marketers, advertisers, and graphic designers come into the mix. They shut down the ugly by turning ingredients into something desirable. After all, no one has ever claimed that people should "have some carbonated water, sugar, caffeine, phosphoric acid, colorants, and flavors—and a smile." But they have claimed that you can "have a Coke and a smile." Marketing professionals focus our attention on the positive features and benefits of the combined ingredients, manufactured beauty, attractive packaging, and artificial emotions.

So is beauty only skin deep?

With people, no, of course not.

But with webinars,

IT IS!

And webinar ugly is one kind of ugly you need to shut down. Because if it looks bad backstage, it will look bad on the runway. There's no magic "dressing room" between bad backstage design and bad runway presentation. Fortunately, the difference between webinar ugly and human ugly is that webinar ugly is easier to fix and doesn't involve surgery, Botox, or squinting. You can shut it down before you take it out in public. Do not be the reason for the ugly.

MEET THE WEBBENY:
Ugly email invitations, ugly marketing, ugly graphics, ugly tweets and posts, ugly presentations, ugly handouts, and ugly webinar experiences. To get a glimpse of this Webbeny, put down the book for a moment and Google "free recorded webinars."

So, what does the "surface" of your webinar look like? This skin is what others see when they log on; it's what they immediately experience once the webinar starts. If what you've got is ugly, don't despair. There's hope.

But in order to shut down webinar ugly, we must `channel`, and in some cases `enlist`, the `help of our friends in marketing, advertising, and graphic design` who have mastered this principle already. We need to become more than instructional designers and presenters; we must evolve, because with webinars, it's imperative that you shut down four ugly touchpoints:

1. Marketing Communication

2. Presentations

3. Handouts

4. Webinar Experiences

1. SHUT DOWN UGLY MARKETING COMMUNICATION

There are a lot of new and innovative ways to invite people to your webinar (social media, microsites) in addition to traditional email and postcards.

Marketing in some form is typically your first webinar touchpoint, and if first impressions make a lasting impact, then some of us are scarred for life. This ugly often appears as an email or a social–media post filled with gobs of text that means nothing to the reader. The typical response to something like this is to delete it. You know what we're talking about. You got half a dozen emails today inviting you to a webinar that you don't care about and we know exactly where they went. Right into your trash. You don't like spam and neither does your audience…

SO STOP IT!

41

Shunning ugly marketing communication will be one of the best things you can do to improve your webinar. At it's foundation, marketing communication is made up of four core skills that are critical to your webinar success.

SKILL #1: FIND BEAUTIFUL BUTTS

You've probably heard someone ask you who your target market is. The term "target market" is loosely defined as "the right butts you want to get in your seats." Not just any butt, you want the `beautiful` butts in seats. If your webinar is supposed to be for people in the music industry, you don't want to waste time and money getting airline pilots or graphic designers or cobblers to attend. You need to stay laser-focused on who you are trying to reach with your webinar.

To help you find the `beautiful` butts, you need to understand more about these people and their needs. Answering a few questions will help you figure this out, and using the following tool is a perfect place to start.

Armed with this information, you will start to understand what your target market looks like.

TARGET MARKET IDENIFICATION TOOL

STEP 1: IDENTIFY WHO THEY ARE.

Age Range:

Gender: ____ % Male ____ % Female

Average Income:

What industries?

What geographic location(s)?

Why do they currently buy from you?

What segment of your current customers brings in the most business?

If you don't have any customers, who is buying from your competitors?

STEP 2: ASK WHY ANYBODY WOULD WANT TO ATTEND THIS WEBINAR.

To solve a problem. What problem?

To satisfy a basic need. What need?

To make themselves feel good. How?

STEP 3: EVALUATE THAT THIS IS THE RIGHT TARGET MARKET.

If you answer no to any of these questions, reevaluate steps 1 and 2.

Can I really reach these people and communicate my message to them?   Y / N

Will this group benefit from my product?   Y / N

Is this group of people big enough to worry about?   Y / N

Can this group afford my product?   Y / N

43

SKILL #2: WRITE BEAUTIFUL WORDS

An effective email is so good looking, you never want to delete it; in fact, you want to share it with others. The same goes for Facebook posts and tweets. They're good looking right from the start. The subject line matches the need of the reader. The imagery sparks the right emotion. The copy is succinct yet informative. It begs you to click on the "register" link.

It doesn't matter how funny or clever your subject line is in an email or how pithy your tweet is if it doesn't relate to the needs of your audience. You must understand your readers' need and whether or not the webinar topic you're offering them meets that interest. If it's not something they need, you risk your webinar being labeled as spam with a consequent loss of interest and trust—which translates to

"I'LL IMMEDIATELY DELETE THE NEXT EMAIL YOU SEND TO ME."

You don't have time to read an essay and neither do we. So keep it simple. Start with a very clear value proposition. What is a value proposition? It's a concise statement that describes why anyone should or would (rather than must or could) attend your webinar. It should focus on results and introduce solutions to a problem the reader has. We really like the way Geoffrey Moore outlines the structure of value propositions in his book *Crossing the Chasm* (Crossing the Chasm: Marketing and Selling High-Tech Products to Mainstream Customers. Geoffrey A. Moore. Published by Harper Business, 1999.), which we recommend you read after this book! Moore states that there are specific points you need to craft into your value proposition, and he has created a simple fill-in-the-blank formula where you just provide short sentences. We've modified it a bit to work for webinars:

For _____
(your target market)

Who are dissatisfied with _____
(their current options)

_____

This webinar provides _____
(the problem you are going to solve)

_____

_____

Unlike _____
(their alternatives)

_____

We have created _____
(key features of your service)

_____

_____

Here's an example:

For   new project managers

Who are dissatisfied with long training courses
to refresh their skill-set,

This webinar provides a two-hour, highly intensive
workshop to share the best practices of seasoned
project managers who have gone before you.

Unlike multi-day workshops where you have to travel
away from your office,

We have created a course where you can avoid the
hassles of travel and still get the best professional
advice available.

Your value proposition needs to contain the beautiful words—the hook—to get them to read more. Write it so that it can be used as a tweet (140 characters) or a post for other social media. You'll also want to provide one or two additional short paragraphs to talk about session details. These can be used as copy in an email and on your registration page. We also recommend three short bullet points to summarize exactly what they'll learn—the benefits—from this webinar. And we must say, don't forget the basics like date and time.

SKILL #3: DESIGN BEAUTIFUL GRAPHICS

WE'RE NOT ALL GRAPHIC DESIGNERS. HOWEVER, DESIGN COUNTS!

To help you create good-looking email templates and registration pages, there are a lot of great online templates for you to use. Just do a search for "effective email templates" or check out sites like constantcontact.com or verticalresponse.com. If you want to get super OCD about all of this—for instance, if you should put graphics on the left or right—follow the principle of Connect or Die. There are so many people who have done A/B testing on the way their landing pages and email campaigns look that they may have the answer you're looking for.

Here are some basic design principles you should consider before sending your email:

- Keep your font size large enough to read comfortably.

- Use complementary colors—make sure they don't clash. A great online tool is colorschemedesigner.com, which will help even the most color-challenged designer.

- Clearly state the date, time, and duration of your webinar.

- Include a call to action ("Register Now!") with a conspicuous register button.

- Use a well-designed masthead (the top of your email).

- Don't include a photo of yourself unless you are a celebrity or it was taken by a professional photographer.

- Don't use too many fonts (only one for the headline and one for the body copy).

When you're done creating your materials (emails, Web pages, Facebook profile page), be sure to "crowd source" it. Show it all to friends, colleagues, and others with whom you have connections and ask for their objective opinions. Make necessary modifications and go away for a day. Don't look your designs for a while. Give yourself some space. The next day, open up them up and give them the gut check: Would you want to read your own email or visit your registration page?

IF NOT, FIX IT.

Finally, proofread your text. Twice. If there are typos, you lose credibility with your readers and they may think the quality of your upcoming webinar will be equally as poor.

UGLY email example:

Our Courses are what you need when you need them.

We have 2 years of excellent reviews from customers. Our goal is to provide you with quality first. We want you to have the project management tools necessary for success. We have enhanced our knowledge base and incorporated adult learning techniques. Your training will be the best! We have the best instructors who have worked with a lot of clients in government agencies, specializing in agricultural agencies.

There are a lot of other project management training companies. But we are different becasue we will help you every step of the way. We will provide a lot of experience plus our prices are competitive. Our instructor has an MBA and has taught dozens of classes with very good reviews!

Our next workshop will be on July 15 at 11:00. If you need more information you can call us at 603-555-1776 or you can visit our website at http://www.improvepmskills.org. We hope to see you in our webinar!

What we offer:
- Thought provoking training
- enhanced competencies
- the latest practices!

48

GOOD email example:

improve
your project management skills

Are you a new project manager but really turned off by long courses to learn project management skills? This two-hour webinar provides a highly interactive experience to learn best practices of the most seasoned project managers.

You will learn the fundamentals of project management directly from PMI certified instructors who will teach you to:
> manage a project through each stage of the life cycle
> develop a project that balances scope, time, and cost
> establish project controls to ensure a success

2-hour Webinar
Friday, July 15
11 am Eastern Time
Price = $199

Space is limited.
Click here to register today!

For more information, contact us at 603-555-1776 or at improvepmskills.org.

EMAIL TIP

Many marketing experts also warn that not everyone uses HTML email. So be sure to also include a text email invitation.

Remember to keep it simple.

49

SKILL #4: USE BEAUTIFUL CHANNELS

You now know your target market (beautiful butts)—the people who you want to attend your webinar. You've created a value proposition (beautiful words) that should pique their interest and persuade them to attend. You've used templates to design beautiful graphics. The last step is to identify the right communication vehicles (beautiful channels).

Before you start production of a 30-second Super Bowl commercial, look closely at your current resources and contacts. You may already have a treasure trove of potential clients tucked away in your email database or an army of followers on social media. If you don't, you need to set a goal to build these databases with potential users. You should consider using a variety of different channels to find followers and communicate your message, because your target market gets their information from so many different places.

Take time right now to evaluate your current databases and set your goals.

Database-Builder Tool			
SOURCES	TODAY'S FOLLOWERS (#)	MY GOAL (#)	BY WHEN
Twitter			
Facebook			
LinkedIn			
Pinterest			
Instagram			
Blog			
Email Lists			
Other:			
TOTAL FOLLOWERS/CONTACTS			

Now think about how you can reach outside your current circle of friends. Some of your followers may actually be willing to repost information about your upcoming webinar—especially if you offer them free admission or are willing to repost something for them in the future. Figure out which followers/friends have the highest value by looking at the quantity of their followers. (Unfortunately it's harder to determine the quality of their followers.)

You should also look outside your circle of friends as well and find thought leaders, authors, and well-read bloggers in your target industry. Don't be afraid—they won't bite.

Reach out to them and ask if they'd be interested in promoting your session. And, LIKE YOUR MAMA ALWAYS SAID, don't forget to tell them, "THANK YOU" if they do.

Keep track of these contacts and commitments here:

Contacts and Commitments Reminder Tool

FOLLOWER/FRIEND/ THOUGHT LEADER	WHAT SOCIAL NETWORK ARE THEY FROM?	THEIR FOLLOWERS (#)	DATE THEY WILL REPOST INFO	MY RETURN COMMITMENT TO THEM
TOTAL FOLLOWERS/CONTACTS				

51

Many people just blast out communication to their targets in an unorganized, pell-mell fashion. UGLY. When you take an organized approach, you will find that you will be less prone to forget things. You will stress less and increase your effectiveness. There are many ways to keep track of the whats and whens. This simple tool can help:

Campaign Scheduling Tool

MEDIA	SIX WEEKS BEFORE	FIVE WEEKS BEFORE	FOUR WEEKS BEFORE	THREE WEEKS BEFORE	TWO WEEKS BEFORE	FIVE DAYS BEFORE	FOUR DAYS BEFORE	THREE DAYS BEFORE	TWO DAYS BEFORE
Example:									
# of Blog Posts	2	2	1	1	1	1	1	1	1
# of Tweets	5	5	5	5	5	1	1	1	2
# of Facebook Posts	2	2	2	2	2	1	1	1	2
# of Email Blasts	1	0	0	0	1	0	1	0	0

TIPS FOR BEAUTIFUL SOCIAL MEDIA

Facebook, Twitter, LinkedIn, and other social-networking sites are fast becoming a proven way to invite people to your webinars. It's fast and easy, but it can also be intrusive and obnoxious. How many followers have you defriended because their posts are the same thing, over and over again. Ugh! There are four simple steps to avoid becoming a Twit or a Facebook Flooder.

1. Use compelling copy (not too slimy) that offers a realistic promise (informative but not dull). For instance, a post that says, "This is the ultimate product for your business. Learn more on our webinar!" is neither compelling nor realistic. Base your post on the value proposition you just created.

2. Don't post it more than three or four times a week and never multiple times a day. Your followers don't want to get spammed, especially if it's something they don't care about. So think before you post. Also, try posting at different times of the day and experiment to see when your followers are most active online.

3. Try posts with different benefit statements. Besides appealing to different user needs, you can use this as an experiment to see which messages resonate more (or less) with your followers. You may even consider using this information to help modify your webinar.

4. Ask influencers and key followers to kindly repost your message. This will help reach a vastly larger audience and increase your credibility. As a thank-you, you should offer to return the favor some day.

53

UGLY Twitter example:

Improve PM Skills @improvepmskills   9 Jun
Our Courses are what you need when you need them. Our webinar is
for beginning PM's. Our goal is to provide you with quality first. We
want...

GOOD Twitter example:

Improve PM Skills @improvepmskills   9 Jun
Learn the 5 secrets behind the best project managers (free webinar).
bit.ly/QH0CpV

2. SHUT DOWN UGLY PRESENTATIONS

We know that a majority of people are visual learners. Unfortunately, one of the biggest mistakes designers make is putting up cruddy-looking slides. One may say that beauty is in the eye of the beholder, but ugly makes everyone shut their eyes. So take a little time or spend a couple of bucks (you can hire a designer for $25/hour) to make your visual design as good as your instructional design.

PowerPoints have typically been built upon a predesigned template loaded with bullets and an image (if you're lucky).

IT'S TIME TO BREAK AWAY FROM THE SAME OLD JUNK.

THINK OUTSIDE THE SLIDE DECK...

BE CREATIVE WITH HOW YOU "TELL" OR "SHOW" THE STORY.

ANTI-UGLY PRESENTATIONS:

1. Throw out tradition.

PowerPoint templates come in one default size (10 inches by 7.5 inches). Change the size of your slide deck to match your content and to visually mix it up. You could make it tall and skinny or short and wide. Think about it. Have you ever seen a PowerPoint that wasn't the default size? Don't conform.

2. Simple is best.

Not too much... less animation... no sounds... less copy... less mess... simple backgrounds... lots of white space... big, readable fonts... nothing fancy... short, concise sentences (if at all). By the way, if any of you create overly distracting slides with the words zooming on or off or tumbling in any way, shape, or form... we're coming for you!

3. Don't regurgitate your spoken words on a slide.

If you are going to say it, you don't need to have it on the screen. It creates "verbal/visual" interference: "What am I supposed to pay attention to—what I'm seeing or what you're saying?" This is ugly. If you have a lot of information, provide a supplemental handout with the detail instead of busy slides.

4. Don't treat attendees like they are senile.

You don't need the title of the webinar on your slides. If people are in front of a screen, they probably didn't fall into that chair by accident nor were they captured by bad guys, tied up, and forced to watch your presentation. They intended to be there; they're not surprised by what's happening. Don't use headers unless absolutely necessary.

55

5. Mix it up.

Don't be afraid to explore and try something beyond the preset templates (but remember Point 2 and keep it simple). Drop in a large photo or put just one word on the screen. It will help keep your audience awake and attentive. Seth Godin, America's greatest marketer and best-selling author, is the mix-it-up king. He's been known to use hundreds of slides with creative images, minimal text, and big color in his presentations.

6. Culture counts.

Be aware of who your audience is. Some global cultures find significance and meaning in specific colors and imagery. Don't offend because you didn't do your research.

7. Try alternatives to PowerPoint.

If your platform allows it, try things like Prezi or Visual.ly.

WHAT IS PREZI? (PREZI.COM)

"Prezi's zoomable canvas makes it fun to explore ideas and the connections between them. The result: visually captivating presentations that lead your audience down a path of discovery."

WHAT IS VISUAL.LY? (VISUAL.LY)

They use infographics defined as "...data visualizations [that] are shifting the way people find and experience stories, creating a new way of seeing the world of data. They help communicate complex ideas in a clear, compact, and beautiful way, taking deep data and presenting it in visual shorthand."

The "Anti-Going Crazy With Design" Warning:
Don't overdose. You could spend days designing
your PowerPoint with all sorts of baubles
and bangles. Find the middle ground between
traditional boring crud and excessive design. You
don't want to distract, you want to instruct. Too
many flashy design elements could take away from
the intended learning outcomes.

UGLY presentation example:

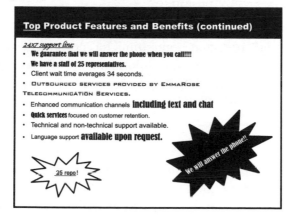

GOOD presentation example:

3. SHUT DOWN UGLY HANDOUTS

Providing some sort of flyer or document that participants can take away with them will ensure they have something to remind them of what they learned during your webinar. Do you want to decrease the likelihood of it getting put on the bottom of the stack of papers on their desk? Make it look nice.

ANTI-UGLY HANDOUT

1. What's your purpose?

Think about what you want people to do with this document—use it as something for notes or learning activities, or use it for information purposes only? Knowing this will help you understand what the design should ultimately look like.

2. What's the content?

It's best to begin by writing down all of your ideas and copy for the handout in a Word or Google document. before spending time on the design. By nature, you will want to do the opposite and start your design first because it's fun. Although you can do minor modifications to your handout design throughout the process, you'll save a ton of time if you have all of the copy written and graphics identified before you start the design. It's hard to do a revamp of your handout after realizing you've unintentionally omitted four important paragraphs. Essentially, that's how we wrote this book. We wrote all of the text in a Google doc where we also identified the graphics we wanted before flowing it into an InDesign document. Try the same thing for your handouts.

3. What does it look like?

There are as many different layout options as... well... there are a lot of them! The secret is to keep it simple and readable. Don't feel like you have to go crazy. Good design is partly self-control.

CONTROL #1: Use only one or two fonts.

CONTROL #2: Use only one or two colors and use them sparingly. As a general rule, pick a base color and a highlight color and remain consistent. Remember, people may be printing this out, so don't empty their color-toner cartridge.

CONTROL #3: Don't use starbursts—ever! They are overused and tacky. You've seen them in poorly designed ads as a bright yellow star to try and get your attention.

CONTROL #4: Use only one image per idea, if needed.

CONTROL #5: Use white space—don't fill up every centimeter with text.

4. SHUT DOWN UGLY WEBINAR EXPERIENCES

With the first three touchpoints, we have applied marketing, advertising, and graphic-design principles. With this last touchpoint, we will return to our instructional-design roots. Because now that we have dressed up and remodeled what our webinar experience looks like (before and during), we need to spend the rest of our time working to get and sustain the attention of our audience.

59

People engage with things they find interesting. Interest is deeper than simply "that's hysterical"—the explanation for why there are so many kitten videos with 100,000 hits on the net. Those videos are not "interesting," they're something less—clever, funny, something to do while I wait for my next meeting. They temporarily draw attention, but for most people, that attention is fleeting.

Getting sustained interest grows out of the concept of "intrinsic motivation," meaning that I, intrinsically or personally, see substantial value in what has just caught my attention. The goal here is to create intrinsic motivation to stay engaged.

WE ARE CREATING WEBINARS, NOT KITTEN VIDEOS!

61

Technology has given webinar designers and presenters a toolkit of "tricks of the trade" that can make our webinars clever, creative, and cool. The most clever, most creative, and coolest webinar that fails to engage people, deliver a message, and affect ongoing behavior is a "kitten video," which may get a lot of hits but won't produce much in the way of important communication and change.

Even when we can grab people's attention and hold on to it by making the content valuable or intrinsically motivating, it is hard to sustain their attention for long.

ANTI-UGLY INSTRUCTIONAL-DESIGN PRINCIPLES

Three types of learning strategies can be incorporated into your instructional design to help get and maintain attention:

1. The 8-Second Rule

People will always struggle to stay focused—even when there's intrinsic motivation. Research tells us a number of things about focus.

First, the average length of time a person can focus on a single idea or stimuli is about 8 seconds (or roughly the time to read one PowerPoint slide with three to four bullet points or to hear the points read back to them or to experience a simple example or illustration of the points).

AFTER 8 SECONDS

(and it took you 8 seconds or more to read that last rambling sentence),

WE CHECK OUT.

If what we just experienced was "intrinsically motivational," we may refocus and reengage. If I get lost because you took more than 8 seconds to get and keep my interest on the first slide, you'll likely not get me back for the second slide. So… whether I'm seeing it, experiencing it, or hearing it, you've got 8 seconds.

By keeping each point to 8 seconds or less and "stacking" those 8-second experiences into a stream of information tied to the audience, their needs and their need for us will increase the chance that they'll stay with us and not check out or power up their smartphones.

2. The 20-Minute Max Rule

Interested and experienced learners can teach themselves to stay focused for as long as 20 minutes (although they are constantly checking in for value and either reengaging or checking out, depending on how the value test goes).

What the 20-Minute Max Rule means to a webinar designer/deliverer is basically this: you've got 20 minutes to get the job done. Or, if you really need longer, you need a SERIES of 20-minute "meetings" that may be linked by short breaks or other activities that make it clear that "this part's done" before you move on.

One thing our industry regularly reinforces is that people need some sort of activity every five to seven minutes. WE tell people that you actually need something every two to three minutes. These activities help maintain focus and improve engagement. These can include verbal interaction, writing in your toolkit, taking polls, answering questions in a chat pod, and so on.

3. The Magic Number 7

In 1956, George Miller, a psychologist at Princeton University, published a world-changing paper on the capacity of working memory. Dr. Miller had discovered (and his results have been replicated many times over) that the ability to take in, process, and productively use information is limited. The limitation is universal, consistent, and inherent. It is universal in that this limitation is found in all people. It is consistent in that it varies only within a limited amount among all people. It is inherent in that it is not affected by factors such as gender, age, education, race, or environment; it's part of our brain wiring.

A webinar is a "data dump." How well that data sticks and helps participants is affected by the two factors we've already covered: can we capture their interest and can we keep them focused?

The final key is to make sure that whatever they are finding interesting and investing focus in has "take-away" value. The key to that take-away value lies in Dr. Miller's discovery, something he called "The Magic Number 7."

Our working memory capacity lies in a narrow, defined range of 7, plus or minus two items. This means that we can remember somewhere between five (7 MINUS TWO) and nine (7 PLUS TWO) things at a time.

Stop for a moment and think of examples of this rule in process. How many numbers in a North American phone number (not including area code)? Answer: 7. How many letters in the English alphabet (26)? How do we remember 26? Answer: We sing the alphabet in chunks fewer than nine letters). You'll notice this book is comprised of 7 main principles.

Whether designing or delivering information in a webinar, you must not violate the Magic Number 7 Rule or people will forget some of what you're sharing. Chunk up your data dumps into between five and nine segments to make things easy to remember.

THE LAST WORD

Shutting down the ugly is about being creative. Creativity creates engagement. Engagement creates behavior change. Behavior change is what you are after.

Look at your webinar experience holistically and create a beautification plan so that ugly in all its facets is shut down for good.

PUTTING PRINCIPLE TO PRACTICE (KEY SUMMARY POINTS)

It's your job to shut down the ugly at four key touchpoints:

1. Marketing communication:
   a. Find beautiful butts. Find the right people to attend your webinar.

   b. Write beautiful words. Only send out good-looking email, tweets, and posts with clear and concise subject lines and a simple message that has a relevant value proposition.

   c. Design beautiful graphics. Create attractive email templates and registration pages and test them with friends, colleagues, and your online network of friends.

    d. Use beautiful channels. Identify the right communication vehicles to market your webinar.

2. Presentations. Keep your visuals simple, refrain from regurgitating what you say onto the slide, don't use obvious headers or predictable slide approaches, and remember to keep the cultures to which you are presenting in mind.

3. Handouts. If you are going to give your webinar attendees a resource, make sure it has purpose and relevance. Oh, and it cannot be UGLY! Use only a couple of fonts and colors, never use starbursts, provide ample white space, and use only one image per idea.

4. Webinar Experience. Use three learning strategies to help beautify your webinar:

    a. The 8-Second Rule. Break up your content chunks and timing into 8-second segments in order to engage and re-engage your attendees.

The 20-Minute Max Rule. Your learners can only stay focused for 20 minutes at a time, so chunk up your content into a series of 20-minute "meetings."

    b. The Magic Number 7. In order to help your learners remember the "data dump" that is a webinar, only provide 7 (PLUS OR MINUS TWO) items for them to learn.

MANIFESTO CHRONICLES

Ideas, solutions, and other cool resources

CAPTIVATE
OR ALIENATE

CAPTIVATE OR ALIENATE

Engage your audience & hold them virtually accountable through what they see, hear, & do.

A few years ago we found ourselves in the Netherlands on business. While there, we took a couple of hours to visit the Van Gogh Museum in Amsterdam.

WHAT WE FOUND SURPRISED US.

70

Van Gogh is known for his use of bright colors, dramatic brush strokes, and paint so thick it can look more like toothpaste than paint. Most visitors to the museum today find his work captivating. But it wasn't always so…

Paintings from Van Gogh's early years were dull, dark monotones, mostly painted in greys and browns. Van Gogh's paintings were anything but attractive, and they mostly went unsold. Like his original audience, we weren't big fans either of his early works.

When Van Gogh painted what would become one of his famous works, The Potato Eaters, in 1885, he thought he had created a masterpiece. His family and friends disagreed. His brother Theo, an art dealer in Paris, wrote to him saying that he was alienating the public and his patrons.

Van Gogh headed to Paris where he sought inspiration from other painters such as Paul Gauguin and Claude Monet.

He learned from their example to paint art that people loved—and bought! He became the Van Gogh that we have come to love.

He left the grays and browns behind and began to paint in color—VIBRANT, POWERFUL, SWIRLING color.

You and your webinar are no different.

Think of yourself as an artist with a technological palette full of color and the potential to create something that will captivate both your fans and your critics.

PULL oʀ PUSH.

LOVE oʀ HATE.

INCLUDE oʀ EXCLUDE.

PROPEL oʀ REPEL.

Learn how to a master your own art in ways that engage and captivate your audience. But also remember to not go overboard with colors. Keep them relevant.

NONVERBAL ACCOUNTABILITY

It's easy to lose someone during a poorly designed and facilitated webinar. Attendees are often sitting in a very distracting environment, and during your webinar, they could be doing anything—emailing, Facebooking, texting their friends.

> **MEET THE WEBBENY:**
> It's critical that you capture your audience quickly and often. Otherwise, like the early Van Gogh, you'll lose or even repel your audience and they'll move on to something they find more engaging, like doing their nails.

In our previous book, *The Learning eXPLOSION: 9 Rules to Ignite Your Virtual Classrooms,* we introduced the concept of nonverbal accountability. In a live event (not a webinar), people are physically present. When you are face-to-face, you can see nonverbal clues from attendees. They signal their level of engagement through overt, physical clues. Positive clues: they raise their hand or nod their head. Negative clues: they start bobbing their head, trying to stay awake.

It's much easier to slip across the line from appropriate to inappropriate behavior in a virtual environment, primarily because these clues can easily go unnoticed. (After all, no one is actually watching.) It's much less likely someone will notice your contribution or your antics—squirreled away in that little box at the top of everyone's screen or represented by a faceless name in an attendee list.

Because both the chance of, and consequences for, getting caught are so small, the temptation to disengage and alienate yourself from the webinar can be great—too great for some to resist.

VIRTUAL ACCOUNTABILITY—MOVING FROM ALIENATING TO CAPTIVATING

Captivating and holding the attention of your webinar participants requires you to find ways to get more than their bodies in front of a terminal. You must get them to attend— and engage. The process of engagement is what we call "virtual accountability" and is comprised of three critical and distinct principles.

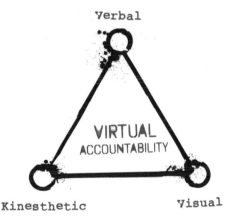

Verbal

VIRTUAL
ACCOUNTABILITY

Kinesthetic   Visual

73

CAPTIVATE PRINCIPLE 1: VERBAL ACCOUNTABILITY— HEAR THEM SPEAK

By now, aren't most of us getting just a little tired of being spectators to our experiences? People have been presenting to us, talking at us, and pushing their content, their ideas, and their perspective forever. How about a revolution—of inclusion—of saying, "I am going to be part of this, or I am going to have none of this."

People are pretty good at figuring out whether they will have a speaking role in the event at hand. Go to a play and it becomes obvious to most people very quickly that the rule is "if you're not on the stage, you don't participate in the talking bits."

Webinars can feel like attending a play where some participants decide, early on, that they are the audience and are to remain silent throughout the process. To create truly memorable and effective webinars, you will want to get the participants out of the audience seats and onto the stage—with speaking parts.

To own their ears and get their mouths to follow, you must stop talking at them and start talking with them, particularly through the use of questions and actions that condition and prompt them to contribute. What follows are activities that generally signal "It's your turn to participate":

1. Set the Stage

At the beginning of the webinar, let participants know that they will be expected to contribute verbally and that they should not mute their phones.

2. Ask Real Questions

Don't ask hypothetical or expected questions—they will kill participation. Ask the kind of questions that stimulate conversations and draw in multiple participants, and once you throw a question out there, let them kick it around for a while.

3. Get Them in Your Sights

There is a concept in cognitive psychology called the "cocktail party effect." Imagine being in a large room with many conversations going on, most of which you're not a part. You quickly learn, in order to concentrate on the task at hand, to ignore the other verbal noise. That is, until your name is called. This is the cocktail party effect—people will always pick up on their name, regardless of whether they are engaged or not. Nothing engages and reengages people like the mention of their name. Use this phenomenon to real effect in your webinar. Call on people by name, bringing the focus to them (give them a second to jump off eBay and log that last bid), but continually reengage them in the process—personally and specifically.

4. Hang 10 (or 15 or 20)

A few seconds of "empty" space on a webinar will feel like an eternity. You must learn to get comfortable with this space—it's critical to engaging people. When you ask a question, give people time to think and answer. Force yourself to give them enough time. We suggest counting to 15. The key: wait as long as you can stand it and then count to 5... that should be about right.

5. Hear the Herd

Some people question the viability of verbal accountability, especially in large webinars. You will hear things like:

"IT'S JUST NOT PRACTICAL
WITH HUNDREDS OF PEOPLE."

"IT WILL BE IMPOSSIBLE TO
MANAGE ALL OF THEIR COMMENTS."

"PEOPLE WILL TALK OVER EACH OTHER."

We disagree. Instead of a brief Q&A section at the conclusion of your webinar, build in multiple opportunities where participants have the chance to talk or chat. If this seems overwhelming, enlist the help of a webinar copilot to help manage the logistics of this exercise.

CAPTIVATE PRINCIPLE 2: VISUAL ACCOUNTABILITY—OPEN THEIR EYES

You all know how hypnosis works—

PICK A SPOT,

   FIXATE ON THAT SPOT,

      LISTEN CAREFULLY TO MY VOICE,

         KEEP LOOKING AT THAT SPOT,

   HEARING MY VOICE,

      YOU'RE GETTING SLEEPY,

         SLEEPY,

            SLEEPIER...

You're now fully relaxed and in my power...

How's that different than "sit there while I talk at you," "look at your screen or that tiny webcam at the top of the screen," "stay focused on that unmoving, text-drenched PowerPoint... and don't feel sleepy, sleepier, sleepier..."

The goal of webinars should not be to induce a hypnotic state. You shouldn't create a "spot" for people to focus on while you lull them into a near-comatose experience. The goal of webinars should be to induce an engaged, interactive, vital state.

Visual accountability is the term we use to describe how to open your participants' eyes—giving them things to look at that are engaging, changing, interesting, and inherently and obviously critical to the meeting at hand.

You can open their eyes and engage participants visually if you remember to include these four key components:

1. Map It

It's as easy to get lost in a meeting or webinar as it is in any unfamiliar neighborhood. Provide a visual map of what's going to happen, where we are now, and where we've been. Just as the best maps have a clearly defined route, they also have clearly defined reference points. (Turn left at the old red barn.) Your webinar map needs road and reference points so people know how far along the journey they are.

2. Paint It

For many people, the ability to see a vivid picture inside their head is as powerful as their desire to experience one outside their own skull. Great storytelling is the key to painting internal pictures. It's also a great way to switch up the process. Instead of loading up one more chart, graph, or YouTube clip, why not paint that chart, graph, or clip inside their head by telling a story? We've been telling each other stories for a long time—as a species, we're primed for good ones—so paint me a picture.

3. Burn It

Not up, but in. Learners are going to expect a PowerPoint presentation filled with text and bullet points. Instead, show them vivid images that teach the concept through graphics rather than text. Most people are visual learners anyway, so not only will it capture their attention, but it will also burn the concept into their mind.

4. Shun It

As in the ugly. If you read Manifesto Principle 3, you know what we mean. If you didn't, read it now.

CAPTIVATE PRINCIPLE 3: KINESTHETIC ACCOUNTABILITY—MOVE THEIR BONES

An object in motion stays in motion. An object at rest stays at rest. If you're not careful, you'll lose any energy that your audience had—unless you get them moving.

Kinesthesia is the study of movement. Webinars tend to ignore movement. They tend to forget that not only do we NEED to move, but that movement can help people learn something new. Grab their arms, move them about, get them moving—literally—and they will get moving—mentally.

The great thing with today's technology is we have so many kinesthetic opportunities. We can...

CLICK, SWIPE, TYPE, MOVE, EXPAND, CONTRACT, SELECT, MAXIMIZE, MINIMIZE...

The list goes on and on. And we can do it by translating physical movement into electronic interaction.

Beyond the physical and kinesthetic realities of the interface opportunities, there are things we can do to virtually engage people at a kinesthetic level. There are three ways to move their bones:

1. Push

Use surveys, polls, chat, and interactive whiteboards to encourage people to push their ideas, input, vision, and concepts into the screen. This will get them moving their mouse, clicking, swiping, selecting, and tapping with the best of them. Don't ever feel like you're overusing these tools. If anything, what we've found is that presenters don't use them enough! People love to share their opinions, and when you give them a way to do so, they stay engaged.

2. Pull

Provide materials for downloading, accessing, visiting... anything that gets them pulling material from the webinar into another environment—real or virtual. The more relevant stuff they pull from the experience, the more stuff they can get their hands on, the more we engage their kinesthetic dimension. You may want learners to do some quick research on a different website, look up a definition, or search for an answer to a question and then return and report to the rest of the group.

3. Play With

Sometimes you need to provide offline assignments—things they can do right now, for just a minute or two. Or things they can do later such as the application of things you're sharing with them. But be sure not to let the offline activity last too long, or you risk losing your audience!

DON'T FORGET STORYTELLING

The principle of captivating an audience is not new. Storytellers have been mastering techniques on how to capture their audience's attention long before webinars or any other modern-day technology.

We should not push aside hundreds of years of best practice and learning just because the modality of gathering people together has changed. Whether sitting by a fireside or logged into a computer, the principles of storytelling still apply.

Human beings are hardwired to remember and retain stories, not to remember and retain bullet points on a slide deck. Think back to the last time you had a PowerPoint presentation thrust at you. Do you remember a list of bullet points? Do you remember what they were? Most likely, you don't remember a single one. Now think about the last story you heard or book you read or movie you watched. Do you remember the story? the characters? the plot? We're confident you can.

In addition to getting our webinar audience to speak, see, and move, we should always look for ways to apply this proven practice in as many aspects of our webinar as possible.

If we want our webinar participants to remember, we must connect with them through effective storytelling.

THE LAST WORD

YOU CAN'T DO IT LIKE YOU USED TO.
THIS MANIFESTO DEMANDS MORE—AN ALTERNATIVE.

Nonverbal accountability—I'm here, you can see me, I nod in the right places and act appropriately—simply doesn't apply to the world of webinars.

We cannot and will not change the webinar world by alienating our audience through the use of traditional face-to-face communication principles. We need to know and apply principles that enable their voices, capture their eyes, and engage their bodies. Your audience needs to feel captivated, inspired, and stimulated by the experience.

One of the best ways to captivate bright people is to draw them out of their seats, through their screens, and into a virtual experience that engages them at multiple levels. We don't need them to sit more; we need them to say more, see more, do more and, in the process, help others say, see, and do more as well. We need them to first, be captivated; second, drawn in; and finally, drawn out—sharing, talking, creating, innovating, and interacting as aggressively in a virtual world just as they would if they were all sitting in the same room together.

REMEMBER, YOU ARE THE ARTIST.

You hold a palette full of technological paints and brushes, but it's up to you to create a masterful piece of art that will captivate the learner. Better still, get them to pick up their own virtual paint and electronic brushes and work alongside you as you collectively create an engaging masterpiece.

PUTTING PRINCIPLE TO PRACTICE (KEY SUMMARY POINTS)

To captivate your virtual audience, you must activate three critical and distinct accountability principles:

Principle 1: Verbal Accountability—
Hear them speak.
Give your participants speaking parts in the webinar.

1. Set the Stage. Establish clear instructions and expectations for verbal interaction.

2. Ask Real Questions. Asking the right questions will stimulate conversations.

3. Get Them in Your Sights. Call them by their individual names.

4. Hang 10. Pause often to give time for content absorption and thought.

5. Hear the Herd. Build in multiple opportunities throughout the webinar for the group to contribute verbally, not just at the end of the webinar.

Principle 2: Visual Accountability—
Open their eyes.

1. Map It. Provide a visual road map of what's going to happen, where we are now, and where we've been.

2. Paint It. Use storytelling to paint the picture.

3. Burn It. Burn the concept into their brains by using vivid images instead of text.

4. Shun It. If it's ugly, change it.

Principle 3: Kinesthetic Accountability—
Move their bones.

1. Push. Use platform tools to involve participants often.

2. Pull. Provide downloadable materials that they pull from the virtual world into their real-life environment, and give them hands-on opportunities to engage.

3. Play With. Let them work offline for very short periods at a time, with clear instructions, and hold them accountable when they return.

Ideas, solutions, and other cool resources

MANIFESTO CHRONICLES

Ideas, solutions, and other cool resources

HUMANIZE THE SCREEN

TWITTER SUMMARY

Get them out. Look @ them, talk 2 them, listen 2 them, & give them room 2 think.

Communication, as we knew it, changed completely between April 1860 and October 1861. And that change passed just south of our offices here at FranklinCovey. The Pony Express, which moved letters and parcels along a 1,900-mile route between St. Joseph Missouri and Sacramento California, allowed people to communicate at a speed unheard of at the time.

A letter posted in California, bordering the Pacific Ocean, could be in downtown St. Joseph in as little as 7 days and 17 hours. The giant expanse of the American continent was fast disappearing. Family and friends—once separated by distance and time—could, with some ease, share the news of the day, knowing it would arrive almost before the week had passed.

Then, in just over 18 months since the day the first rider left Sacramento, the intercontinental telegraph arrived. Then the telephone, then television, then... (you get the idea). Each technology made it both faster and easier to communicate over a great distance. But has the quality of our communication kept pace with the speed and complexity of the technology?

Technological advances shrink space. A webinar makes it possible for people to speak, literally, face-to-face and voice-to-voice across monumental distances. So if we CAN communicate, why do so many webinars feel like we're still a thousand miles apart—if not literally, at least in the way we interact?

> **MEET THE WEBBENY:**
> Talking to a screen and ignoring the person on the other side.

The fifth principle of the Webinar Manifesto seeks one change: We will use webinar technology to interact as if we are literally "face-to-face" or "voice-to-voice."

That change requires that we get beyond the technology and act as if we're in the same room. In the earliest days of the telephone, people struggled to make that technology as natural as a face-to-face conversation. In fact, it took some time to agree on a common way to answer the phone. (Alexander Graham Bell—the inventor—initially proposed "Ahoy.") Now, years later, awkward questions like "how to answer" are long passed—a phone conversation has become, simply, a conversation.

The processes that apply to face-to-face communication apply to webinars. The errors we commit when communicating face-to-face apply webinars. The improvements we can make to face-to-face communication apply to webinars. In other words, we need to...

STOP

emphasizing the technology and the differences (isn't it cool that I can see you way over there in Sri Lanka?) and

START

acting as if we're in the same room.

Because, let's face it, webinars are the new room.

(Disclaimer: We are **NOT** saying that you should replace traditional face-to-face communication. We know that this is still one of the best humanizing forms of communication. No, if you are planning on lunch with a friend or a date with your spouse, don't do it via webinar.)

FACE-TO-FACE, MEET THE NEW F2F

What do you think about when you hear "face-to-face"? You think of one face attached to one person next to another face attached to another person. They're present—physically, if not substantially, but they're there—in the same space, in the same room—them, and their faces—in a setting where they can literally reach out and touch each other (although for HR reasons, they probably shouldn't).

Effective face-to-face communication was defined decades ago by Albert Mehrabian, a renowned psychologist in the field of nonverbal communication. His theories and research have since become the de facto standard. Mehrabian proposed that face-to-face interactions are made up of three elements: (1) people don't just hear the WORDS you say, (2) they also hear the TONE of your voice, (3) and read your BODY LANGUAGE. These three elements are weighted differently in a conversation. As a general rule, the words we use account for just 7 percent of communication, our tone of voice accounts for 38 percent, and our nonverbal behaviors, including facial expressions, account for 55 percent.

7%
WORDS

55%
BODY
LANGUAGE

38%
TONE OF
VOICE

The bulk of Mehrabian's work was published in the 1970s and communication has changed dramatically since the era of bell-bottoms and disco.

The new F2F requires an upgrade to the original Mehrabian philosopy, with a new set of skills.

FOUR HUMANIZING SKILLS

Don't think of webinars as a bunch of disjointed pieces (a computer screen, a webinar platform, and people on the other side). Rather, try and think past the hardware, past the screen. We keep talking about how we live in a virtual world—practice it; go Matrix; get so deep into the machine that you can't tell whether you're in or out of it. Humanize the virtual experience. You can create the new F2F by mastering four humanizing skills.

Skill One- Look at Me

Look at me when I'm talking to you. Adults used to say this to kids all the time. Eye contact is a very intimate and personal human activity. It communicates all kinds of things—interest, concern, attention, empathy… Whether you use a webcam or not, you can command attention. You can figuratively require participants to look at you. This type of online presence comes with practice. It comes with platform proficiency. It comes with understanding the power of your virtual presence.

To understand virtual presence, think of a friend, a family member, a mentor with whom you have a healthy, long-distance relationship. Think of how natural it feels to talk with that person over the phone, or via Skype, or even texting. He or she has your undivided attention and vice versa. You look at each other even when you are not physically looking at each other. You are virtually present. With proper expectations and some practice, you can enjoy the same dynamic with your webinar attendees. Cindy Hugget, a world-class webinar presenter, puts a photo of her husband above her screen to help her feel like she is talking to another human being.

Eye contact is still essential to F2F but now involves focusing attention on the computer screen. After all, it's where eye contact would exist if we were sitting across from each other. It's where—if we were talking or demonstrating something—we'd look. It's the space between us; just a little farther apart than usual. Just as vibrant eye contact helps maintain itself, vibrant screen contact will increase another's willingness to stay focused.

Skill Two- Talk to Me

Some people shout into their cell phones. Some are just loud talkers, like the person sitting next to one of us on a recent flight. We didn't doubt that everyone on the flight heard him tell his wife he had landed and that he had an enjoyable trip. While being around a loud talker can be annoying, being instructed by a loud webinar presenter is much worse.

THERE'S NO NEED TO YELL AT ME!

Sometimes we forget that technology can work well. And when it works well, especially on the audio end, there's no need to yell. Moderate your volume and tone; talk as if the person were right next to you.

Also, watch out for the tendency, especially in extended webinars, to shift into a distant monotone. Remain engaged and signal that engagement in the way you speak.

Let me hear that you're present and interested. In regular, old-fashioned face-to-face speaking, we often adjust our presence to regain focus and personal engagement. We shift in our chairs, we stretch, we stand up, we lean in or out, we use physical movement to gain mental attention. Remember, even though people can't see you, they can feel your energy and attentiveness through your voice and nonverbal actions. This spirit cannot be manufactured, because it's human. It's real. It's who you are. In your webinar, try it—adjust your voice and body to engage, energize, and humanize the experience. (Don't wander off... that's too much adjustment, old or new face-to-face!)

Skill Three- Listen to Me

If you find yourself presenting a webinar, and all you hear is yourself,

SHUT UP.

Just like any in-person face-to-face interaction, it isn't optimal for just one of the parties to keep babbling on. So it is with webinars.

You may be the expert facilitator, the subject-matter expert, but you're not the Great Oz, and they're not mindless robots. Of course it may be your webinar and you may be running it—just don't be ruining it. Physically or virtually, in any form of face-to-face or F2F there needs to be a speaker and a listener. Those roles need to regularly switch and they need to find some reasonable, fluid balance or you don't have a conversation, you have a recital. (And no one is a real fan of recitals—not the second-grade violin kind or the webinar kind.) Take time to listen to what others have to teach YOU. You may be surprised at what you learn. No "talking heads" in the new F2F or you'll start creating "bobbing heads" as your group checks out—and you may never know until someone's head hits the keyboard, followed by a stream of odd text in a chat pod!

Skill Four- Let Me Think

A friend recently stepped off the escalator at the Atlanta Hartsfield Airport and nearly stepped into a great, giant slick of vomit. Some poor kid had just had enough. It wasn't fun for our friend and it REALLY wasn't fun for the kid. Webinar vomit is no fun either. Some people just spin up the webinar and start to hurl—a nonstop stream of talk, talk, talk.

DON'T BOMBARD ME.

If you want me to read something, give me time to read it. Don't talk while I'm reading. Give me time to digest it. If you want me to talk, let me talk—don't butt in, cut me off, talk, or type over me (easy to do on some webinar connections, so wait for the quiet lag). If you ask me to do something or want me to experience something (see it, hear it, experience it, study it), give me time and space to do so. Give me room to think.

To understand how to give someone room to think, it is advantageous to first understand how people process information.

CODING

We talk all the time about sharing ideas or laying out some of "my thoughts." This is nonsense. We're not telepathic, and we can't read each other's mind, which is what thought sharing really is. Thoughts have to be coded.

WORDS are CODE.

PICTURES are CODE.

GRAPHICS and DIAGRAMS are CODE.

EXCEL SPREADSHEETS are CODE
(secret code for some of us!).

The code you select will profoundly affect the ability of the person you're communicating with to get your point across. The challenge lies in the fact that we tend to choose code (words, language, acronyms, diagrams, shortcuts) that is comfortable and clear for US, without thinking about whether it's as accessible to YOU.

Pay attention to WHO you are going F2F with. Make an effort to understand the code they prefer. If, for example, they are not part of your organization, then watch out for company acronyms, jargon, and references to company experience, history, or culture—they'll escape your audience and alienate them from what you want to say.

TRANSMITTING

A webinar is a form of transmitting. Within a webinar are a bundle of transmitting options—show a picture, display a graphic, talk and listen, play an audio clip, look at each other over webcam, share a video.

In Principle 4, "Captivate or Alienate," we outlined the principles that underlie the transmitting challenge. The challenge is simply this: How you prefer to transmit the information may **NOT** be how I prefer to receive the information. Since you want to connect with me, doesn't it make sense to adjust how you transmit so it's more in line with how I choose to receive?

If I'm visual, show me a chart, a graph, a graphic.

If I'm auditory, let's talk or let's listen to something together.

If I like to read complex information rather than hear and discuss, use the webinar to get me the document or send it out in advance with the webinar invitation.

If I'm kinesthetic, get me doing something. (Let me "Google"; let me press some buttons, push some cursors, click up some data.)

DECODING

Once an idea is coded and transmitted, the person at the other end is decoding it—trying to figure out what you're trying to communicate. There are two things you can do to help ensure that decoding works best.

First, give the person time to process the information, in whatever form you've shared it. Get comfortable with silence, the pregnant pause, the 15-second rule. YOU don't need 15 seconds (you've already decoded and processed it in order to be able to present it well), but THEY are getting it for the first time—so chill!

Second, ask questions to confirm comprehension. Don't make the questions juvenile or insulting. Don't make the questions so broad as to be useless—questions such as, "Do you see how we've used triangles to represent the direction of the process?" Instead, try something like, "How do the symbols we've used indicate process direction?" The difference is subtle, but Question 1 may signal that you're not sure they can grasp the basics, whereas Question 2 uses coding—a higher-level concept.

CONFIRMING

Confirming closes the communication loop. You started this F2F interaction by treating it like a face-to-face experience— EYE CONTACT, VOICE MODULATION, PACING. You then focused on coding and transmitting in ways that engage your group rather than, unintentionally, alienating them. Effective, probing questions give you a chance to make sure what you want to say and what they actually experience are very close to the same thing.

Confirming is your chance to open up the conversation. At this level, you are looking for feedback that implies people not only got the message but are now processing it in their own sphere—making connections, offering suggestions, challenging assumptions, talking about application. If people pick up your initial communication and start to do something with it, you have confirmation or evidence that you're connecting at the level you intended.

THE LAST WORD

Mehrabian's rules, that have governed face-to-face conversation—where a person is physically present—have been upgraded to meet the needs of the new F2F. By applying new skills and acting as if everyone's present, you create an environment that acts and feels more like a regular conversation. And in acting as if you're part of a regular conversation, it becomes more real. As conversations become real, the technology moves to the background, and the people—as this manifesto principle asserts—come out of the screen and into the room.

PUTTING PRINCIPLE TO PRACTICE (KEY SUMMARY POINTS)

Create the new F2F (face-to-face) virtual experience by mastering four humanizing skills:

Skill One—Look at Me. Create an online presence where participants feel like they are not looking at a screen but at a human being on the other side of the screen.

Skill Two—Talk to Me. Don't yell, be robotic, or go monotone. Try conversing in regular, old-fashioned face-to-face lingo, as if you were talking with a friend. Be natural. Smile, and don't forget to breathe.

Skill Three—Listen to Me. If all you can hear is yourself, then shut up and listen. In any form of interaction (in person or online), there needs to be a speaker and a listener, and those roles need to switch regularly in order to have a healthy discourse.

Skill Four—Let Me Think. Don't bombard me with information. Give me time to think, process, and reply.

Ideas, solutions, and other cool resources

MANIFESTO CHRONICLES

Ideas, solutions, and other cool resources

CRACK THE FEEDBACK CODE

CRACK THE FEEDBACK CODE

TWITTER SUMMARY

Learn how 2 identify visible & invisible feedback codes & the 4 cyphers used 2 decode them.

In 1820 a treasure of gold, silver, and jewels was allegedly buried by Thomas Jefferson Beale in Bedford County, Virginia. Along with the treasure, Beale provided three cryptograms, or secret codes. The first described the location of the treasure. The second and third described, respectively, the contents of the treasure and the treasure owners' next of kin. Years later, in 1855, the codes were published by James B. Ward in a pamphlet titled *The Beale Papers*.

In the pamphlet, Ward outlined how he cracked the second code using the Declaration of Independence as the key. He realized that each number represented a word in the document and then extracted the first letter. For example, one of the numbers is 73. The 73rd word in the Declaration of Independence is "hold," so you take the first letter of that word "h" to create the solution.

But the other two cryptograms remain locked and unbroken. See if you can unlock Beale's first code.

You could become famously wealthy!

104

71, 194, 38, 1701, 89, 76, 11, 83, 1629, 48, 94, 63, 132, 16,
111, 95, 84, 341, 975, 14, 40, 64, 27, 81, 139, 213, 63, 90,
1120, 8, 15, 3, 126, 2018, 40, 74, 758, 485, 604, 230, 436,
664, 582, 150, 251, 284, 308, 231, 124, 211, 486, 225, 401,
370, 11, 101, 305, 139, 189, 17, 33, 88, 208, 193, 145, 1, 94,
73, 416, 918, 263, 28, 500, 538, 356, 117, 136, 219, 27, 176,
130, 10, 460, 25, 485, 18, 436, 65, 84, 200, 283, 118, 320,
138, 36, 416, 280, 15, 71, 224, 961, 44, 16, 401, 39, 88, 107,
304, 12, 21, 24, 283, 134, 92, 63, 246, 486, 682, 7, 219, 184,
360, 780, 18, 64, 463, 474, 131, 160, 79, 73, 440, 95, 18, 64,
581, 34, 69, 128, 367, 460, 17, 81, 12, 103, 820, 62, 116, 97,
103, 862, 70, 60, 1317, 471, 540, 208, 121, 890, 346, 36, 150,
59, 568, 614, 13, 120, 63, 219, 812, 2160, 1780, 99, 35, 18,
21, 136, 872, 15, 28, 170, 88, 4, 30, 44, 112, 18, 147, 436,
195, 320, 37, 122, 113, 6, 140, 8, 120, 305, 42, 58, 461, 44,
106, 301, 13, 408, 680, 93, 86, 116, 530, 82, 568, 9, 102, 38,
416, 89, 71, 216, 728, 965, 818, 2, 38, 121, 195, 14, 326, 148,
234, 18, 55, 131, 234, 361, 824, 5, 81, 623, 48, 961, 19, 26,
33, 10, 1101, 365, 92, 88, 181, 275, 346, 201, 206, 86, 36,
219, 324, 829, 840, 64, 326, 19, 48, 122, 85, 216, 284, 919,
861, 326, 985, 233, 64, 68, 232, 431, 960, 50, 29, 81, 216,
321, 603, 14, 612, 81, 360, 36, 51, 62, 194, 78, 60, 200, 314,
676, 112, 4, 28, 18, 61, 136, 247, 819, 921, 1060, 464, 895,
10, 6, 66, 119, 38, 41, 49, 602, 423, 962, 302, 294, 875, 78,
14, 23, 111, 109, 62, 31, 501, 823, 216, 280, 34, 24, 150,
1000, 162, 286, 19, 21, 17, 340, 19, 242, 31, 86, 234, 140,
607, 115, 33, 191, 67, 104, 86, 52, 88, 16, 80, 121, 67, 95,
122, 216, 548, 96, 11, 201, 77, 364, 218, 65, 667, 890, 236,
154, 211, 10, 98, 34, 119, 56, 216, 119, 71, 218, 1164, 1496,
1817, 51, 39, 210, 36, 3, 19, 540, 232, 22, 141, 617, 84, 290,
80, 46, 207, 411, 150, 29, 38, 46, 172, 85, 194, 39, 261, 543,
897, 624, 18, 212, 416, 127, 931, 19, 4, 63, 96, 12, 101, 418,
16, 140, 230, 460, 538, 19, 27, 88, 612, 1431, 90, 716, 275,
74, 83, 11, 426, 89, 72, 84, 1300, 1706, 814, 221, 132, 40,
102, 34, 868, 975, 1101, 84, 16, 79, 23, 16, 81, 122, 324, 403,
912, 227, 936, 447, 55, 86, 34, 43, 212, 107, 96, 314, 264,
1065, 323, 428, 601, 203, 124, 95, 216, 814, 2906, 654, 820,
2, 301, 112, 176, 213, 71, 87, 96, 202, 35, 10, 2, 41, 17, 84,
221, 736, 820, 214, 11, 60, 760.

Over the decades, there have been many attempts to find the Beale treasure. One woman even dug up a cemetery looking for the gold and jewels. But in the end, everyone has given up, disappointed. If they only had the key—the cypher to crack the first code—then it would be a breeze.

UNDERSTANDING THE CODES

Many of us have taught webinars that felt like a frustrating (and often futile) search for "lost treasure"—looking for feedback from attendees to help us understand if anyone actually learned something. Just as with gold and jewels, webinars can either keep people from or lead them to the treasure the experience offers.

106

The differentiating factor seems to be:
CODES.

We've uncovered two types of codes related to webinar feedback: visible and invisible. When you understand them—and crack them—you will gain a treasure trove of valuable information that can power up the next webinar, making it a substantially better experience.

Visible codes are relatively easy to decrypt and don't require a cypher, or key. You find these codes in the formal feedback obtained from attendees after the session. Reviewing the insights coded in formal feedback is not new to most of us. There is little skill required to read a feedback form. The challenge comes in implementing what you read—it takes time, you don't agree with some of what is said, you don't have budget to make the fix. There's always a reason not to engage with the feedback—to ignore the visible code and, in doing so, lose a chance to gather some real treasure.

The more difficult codes to crack are the invisible ones. This is where you should spend time, honing your code-breaking skills. Invisible codes are hidden in the cryptic behaviors of your participants—before, during, and after the session.

HOW TO BECOME AN INVISIBLE-CODE BREAKER

Have you ever played one of those little handheld games that involve moving some tiny metal balls around a pathway inside a clear plastic container? There are targets, in the form of tiny pockets or indentations; and pathways, in the form of edges, corners, and bumpers. Your task is to take the little toy in both hands and try to manipulate one or more of the tiny metal balls into some sort of scoring position. Usually, what happens is the minute you get one ball nestled in its target indentation and start to move the second ball, the first one rolls free and everything starts all over.

Success in the game requires that you pay attention to every ball in the game—you can't assume that the ball(s) nestled in scoring position will stay there. Nor can you take your eye off the ball in play or it will never get to its intended position. Nor can you be too gentle or too rough. Don't move the toy enough and nothing moves forward; move it too aggressively and all the balls go flying. This is not easy stuff. (We think that's why most of these games are little, inexpensive toys—that way it doesn't matter when you throw the thing at the wall.)

The secret to success in the game lies in the ability to balance input (how you tilt the game, how softly or aggressively you proceed, which ball you move

107

first, second, etc.) against the feedback the game provides—what can you see, feel, hear—and what that feedback is telling you. Move it too quickly in one direction and all the balls scatter; but tilt it "just so" and you can hold one ball in place and, by flicking another corner with your finger—very softly—the next ball can be coaxed to its target.

WATCH, MOVE, FEEDBACK...

WATCH, MOVE, FEEDBACK...

GENTLY, SLOWLY, NOW HARD...

NOW FAST, TOO FAR...

BACK OFF...

Chatter is feedback. Questions, conversations, challenges—interaction of any kind or type is feedback. Waiting until the end of a webinar to ask the typical and mostly useless question, "So how did that work for everyone?" is like playing the little toy game blindfolded, with ear muffs and mittens on.

IT'S A TOTAL CRAPSHOOT.

Push your premise, your anticipated outline, your main points out early. Get people talking about them, tweeting about them, and feeding that talk and those tweets back to you. Know early and know lots about whether your webinar is designed to succeed or doomed to fail. Then incorporate that feedback—aggressively. If you're way off course, work to get way "on" course.

If the TWEETS
ask for TWEAKING,

then TWEAK

109

in favor of
the TWEETS.

THE 4 CODES AND CYPHERS

Every webinar is governed by four codes, founded in four questions, that you need to crack. These are questions that are rarely asked and that can leave dangerous invisible codes—like Trojans or keyloggers—just below the surface of what you think is going on. They are the kind of questions learners ask themselves inside their heads, because, if asked out loud, they might appear rude, even if they're accurate.

> **MEET THE WEBBENY:**
> Avoiding, ignoring, and discounting feedback before, during, and after the webinar experience.

INVISIBLE CODE #1: POOR ATTENDANCE

This invisible code precedes the webinar. It's triggered by the invitations. You send one out to a thousand people and 20 sign up. What was the cause for such a low sign-up rate?

Attendees are looking at the webinar invitation and then at their schedule, realizing how little room is left for "one more thing." It's the question of value for investment: "If I put this in my schedule—which is already crammed full for Wednesday—will it be worth it? Will the time invested and the value received be a fair or even profitable exchange, or am I about to get cheated out of another valuable hour of my time?"

CYPHER #1

A webinar is not a given. It is a product, an experience, an online offer. It must, like everything else that has a chance to succeed online or offline, be marketed. Your marketing needs to answer these three questions:

`Market`

`Are you inviting the right people?` If not, how can you find the right people?

`Message`

`Does your webinar offer something they want? at the right price? at the right time?` If not, test your message with a sample group of your intended audience to make sure your value proposition is dead on. Answers to these questions provide invaluable information. It creates an opportunity for people to respond to what they're signing up for. It's their chance to challenge what you want to cover in the context of what they need to cover. It's their chance to insert themselves into the process early on and to assure themselves that they're being heard and included. It helps them start to believe "this `WILL` be worth it."

`Media`

`Are you reaching people in the right way? at the right time?` Maybe the skywriting campaign on Miami Beach isn't the best way to reach your audience. Perhaps an effective email campaign (based on the "Shut Down the Ugly" principle) would be better.

Using an online analytics tool such as Google Analytics (which is free!) can help you crack the first invisible code. You'll be able to measure the effectiveness of your invitation and registration page by showing how many people viewed and completed it. The tools below will help you find areas of improvement.

How strong is your campaign? Did anyone even visit your registration page? If not, are you reaching the right people, or does your message need to be tweaked?

Campaign Response Rates

DATE OF POST/EMAIL	SOURCE	# PEOPLE TARGETED	# PEOPLE WHO VISITED REGISTRATION PAGE	RESPONSE RATE (# VISITS/# TARGETED)
Example: August 8	My Twitter Followers	8,539	256	3%

If your registration rates are low, examine your registration page. Is it too complicated? Is there too much information? Is the message inconsistent with the communication that led people there? Is your price too high?

Registration Rates

# PEOPLE WHO VISITED REGISTRATION PAGE	# PEOPLE WHO REGISTERED	REGISTRATION RATE (# REGISTERED/# VISITED)
Example: 256 visits	15	5.9%

If you had low attendance to your webinar, do you know why? We've found that if you are offering a free webinar, you can typically expect a 50 percent no-show rate.

Attendance Rates

TOTAL # PEOPLE REGISTERED	# PEOPLE WHO ATTENDED WEBINAR	ATTENDANCE RATE (# ATTENDED/# REACHED)
Example: 15	12	80%

Now, take time to reflect on your results. Learn from what you've done so that you can improve next time.

Using this cypher to crack this first invisible code will get your intended attendees to exclaim,

"THIS WILL BE WORTH IT."

INVISIBLE CODE #2: DROPOFF

So you hooked me on "Will this be worth it?" and I'm here—I'm online, I'm logged in. Now you need to make sure I'm not thinking,, "Have I made a mistake; is this worth it?"

This question floats through any webinar that's not clicking. Learners may have convinced themselves, when they accepted the email invitation, that this might be a good opportunity.

But now that the session's underway, they're starting to lose faith: "Maybe this was a bad idea. Can I jump off the call? If not, will they hear me typing? Or maybe I could surf the Web on my tablet or smartphone. That's the great thing about a nonmechanical keyboard: no click-click for others to hear. Or I can start on that document that's due this afternoon and have them think I'm just taking notes."

CYPHER #2

Dropoff has a direct correlation to design and delivery. If you nail these concepts, people will stick around. Many of the principles in this book will help you crack this code; specifically, "Don't Default," "Shut Down the Ugly," "Captivate or Alienate," and "Humanize the Screen."

INVISIBLE CODE #3: SILENCE

During your webinar, you will have identifiable moments when key points are being made, key questions are being asked, or key interactions are being launched. These are the times to seek feedback because these are the moments when the webinar message either connects or disconnects. These are the moments when people either engage and interact, or disengage and surf—when they ask themselves, "Does my opinion matter?"

CYPHER #3

Silence means a few things might be going on here:

Technical—They can't engage. Check that video, audio (they are on mute), chat, etc., is up and working. Start with the simplest barrier and work up.

Traditional—Have you, your webinar, or your organization created a tradition of "talking heads" interacting with "nodding heads"? Have you, in the past, encouraged participation?

Terror—Is it safe to engage? Sometimes people don't engage because past experience (even if it's not directly with you) has proven that talking is a career-limiting move and not an acceptable webinar practice.

Too much—of you. Are you talking instead of, in spite of, over the top of, or to the exclusion of others? Remember, this is a webinar, not a sermon.

Too fast—Are you pausing, allowing time for people to formulate a response, comment, challenge, or question? Remember, a few seconds of silence can feel like eternity. Count it down.

Too soon—Have you laid enough groundwork at this point for people to feel comfortable responding or commenting? They may be waiting for more context or content before they jump in.

INVISIBLE CODE #4: NO FEEDBACK

Okay, they accepted the invite, they're done with the webinar, the time is spent: "Was this worth it? Have I got some ideas, some insights, some tools and information that will help me, or was this another lost hour? Did the webinar work for me? Did it include me? Was I heard? Did I get the time to make my points, or do I feel like I've just finished drinking from a PowerPoint firehose where all I can remember is...

THAT WAS A LOT OF SLIDES?!"

As your webinar wraps up, you have an opportunity to seek the first-level input on "Was this worth it?" We recommend getting people to reply to this immediately—even during the session. If you can't get feedback before everyone leaves, you should send follow-up emails or questionnaires, although it takes more time and participation is often lower than expected.

CYPHER #4

There are three separate parts to this cypher:

No Feedback Submitted—Find out why: "The process was too confusing, too complicated, too time-consuming, didn't give me a way to say what I wanted to say." Maybe you didn't allow time for feedback. Generally, people want feedback time wrapped into the total webinar time; otherwise, you're asking for additional time on their schedule—which may not work for them.

Spotty Submissions—Talk to submitters. Why did they choose to submit? Talk to non-submitters. Why did they choose not to? Did you give them proper instructions? Was the feedback tool easy to use?

Box Checkers Only—Was the survey too time-consuming? Were the scales sufficiently representative of the feedback? Did participants think their comments would have little or no effect? Is the "Comments" section engaging—does it ask for comments in specific areas? (Tell us what the best interaction event was in the webinar. Where did you feel too much/too little time was spent?) Or is it just the traditional, boring "comments" followed by cavernous white space that seems better-suited to doodling than commenting?

Feedback Cracking Tool

Contact three of your webinar attendees and ask them the following:

INVISIBLE CODE #1: "POOR ATTENDANCE"

1. What was it about the webinar invitation that made you sign up—to solve a problem, to satisfy a basic need, or to make you feel good? Why?

Attendee 1

Attendee 2

Attendee 3

2. Was the webinar invitation compelling enough? If not, how would you improve it?

Attendee 1

Attendee 2

Attendee 3

INVISIBLE CODE #2: "DROPOFF"

3. Did you multitask during the webinar (e.g., check email)? Why?

Attendee 1- Y / N, Why?

Attendee 2- Y / N, Why?

Attendee 3- Y / N, Why?

INVISIBLE CODE #3: "SILENCE"

4. Did you feel the webinar was a safe environment in which to collaborate and comment? Why?

Attendee 1- Y / N, Why?

Attendee 2- Y / N, Why?

Attendee 3- Y / N, Why?

5. Did you feel like you were engaged throughout the webinar? Give an example of how.

Attendee 1- Y / N, How?

Attendee 2- Y / N, How?

Attendee 3- Y / N, How?

6. Was the content delivered in a way that you could easily follow (e.g., with a clear road map or agenda)?

Attendee 1- Y / N

Attendee 2- Y / N

Attendee 3- Y / N

INVISIBLE CODE #4: "NO FEEDBACK"

7. Was the webinar worth it? Why?

Attendee 1- Y / N, Why?

Attendee 2- Y / N, Why?

Attendee 3- Y / N, Why?

8. Did you complete and submit the feedback form at the end of the webinar? If not, why not?

Attendee 1- Y / N, Why not?

Attendee 2- Y / N, Why not?

Attendee 3- Y / N, Why not?

THE LAST WORD

Everybody knows the importance of gathering honest feedback. Maybe we've never thought about gathering it before, during, and after as a tactic to minimize the impact of the invisible codes and maximize the power of the visible codes. We all know, as *The Webinar Manifesto* states, that we need feedback—the kind you can see and hear, not the kind you wonder about and worry about.

Feedback doesn't always go our way. Sometimes the webinar we poured

BLOOD,
SWEAT,
TEARS,
AND TIME INTO FALLS FLAT.

Sometimes feedback hurts; even if it helps, it hurts. So... we avoid it. After all, we all have a primitive part of our brain that, when threatened, triggers our fight-or-flight response. And since fighting usually ends up with a visit to HR (and maybe the ER), we more often flee—we fail to seek the feedback, read the feedback, or do anything about it. We just agree not to spend time with each other.

This is one of those principles in *The Webinar Manifesto* that's not quite as fun as "Shut Down the Ugly" or quite as mechanical as "Cage the Monsters" or quite as fascinating as "Captivate or Alienate." This one is hard to do and, sometimes, hard to take. But it can have tremendous value.

Because when you find feedback and take it in, then make the necessary modifications, something critical changes. The webinar stops being YOUR class and starts being OUR class. And as YOURS morphs into OURS, people engage—in planning the next one, in participating in the next one, and in putting to work the ideas our webinar generated. And things get better...

FOR ALL OF US.

PUTTING PRINCIPLE TO PRACTICE (KEY SUMMARY POINTS)

To effectively crack the feedback code, you cannot just rely on visible feedback codes like feedback forms and Q&A, usually placed at the end of a webinar. You must also learn to understand and decipher four invisible feedback codes:

Invisible Code #1: Poor Attendance

This invisible code is usually caused by poor webinar invitations, including a bad value proposition, BEFORE the actual event. To help people realize that "YES! It will be worth it," every marketing invitation you send should answer three questions.

1. Market. Are you inviting the right people?

2. Message. Does your webinar offer something they want? at the right price? at the right time?

3. Media. Are you reaching people in the right way? at the right time?

Invisible Code #2: Dropoff

Once your participants are LOGGED IN to the webinar, they are constantly asking themselves, "Is this really worth my time?" If it's not, they'll drop off. If it is, they'll stay on a little longer. To ensure the webinar experience meets and exceeds expectations, you should have already applied other principles from the book, including "Don't Default," "Shut Down the Ugly," "Captivate or Alienate," and "Humanize the Screen." Because once they are in the webinar, it is too late to design a better experience.

Invisible Code #3: Silence

Silence DURING a webinar can be attributed to a few causes:

- **Technical.** They can't engage—for some reason they are on mute or disconnected from the session.

- **Traditional.** They have been conditioned to NOT talk because of previous "talking head" experiences.

- **Terror.** They don't feel comfortable contributing in the webinar environment for whatever reason.

- **Too much...** of you. Remember, lectures and sermons are typically given to a silent audience.

- **Too fast.** Pause and allow for responses, comments, challenges, and thought.

- **Too soon.** You need to provide context and content before attendees will participate.

Invisible Code #4: Poor Feedback or No Feedback Scores

As your webinar is **WRAPPING UP,** seek input from your participants immediately, before they check out and log off. If they do leave the webinar, try contacting them afterward via email or phone or questionnaire to receive clarity on the following three feedback behaviors:

1. **No Feedback Submitted.** Was it too confusing? too complicated? too long?

2. **Spotty Submissions.** Did you give them proper instructions? Was the tool too hard to use?

3. **Box Checkers Only.** Was the survey too time-consuming? Did they think their comments would have little or no effect?

Ideas, solutions, and other cool resources

CAGE THE MONSTERS

CAGE THE MONSTERS

🐦 TWITTER SUMMARY

Webinars can be deadly—for your webinar—if you don't cage the content, technology, & delivery monsters.

The most deadly monster in Greek mythology was Typhon. Known as the father of all monsters, he was one of the largest and most fearsome creatures.

EVEN THE GODS FEARED TYPHON.

As legend goes, Typhon was intent on destroying Zeus, the father of all gods, because Zeus had imprisoned the Titans. In their first battle, Typhon bettered Zeus, tearing out his sinews. Hermes recovered the sinews and restored them to Zeus who, now healed, returned to his battle with Typhon. This time, Zeus triumphed and buried Typhon underneath Mount Etna.

You probably have no monsters in your life quite as threatening as the hundred-headed Typhon.

Your WEBINAR MONSTERS may be different, BUT JUST AS DEADLY.

They are far less scary at first, maybe because they only have three heads—Content, Technology, and Delivery.

> **MEET THE WEBBENY:**
> Disorganized content, unprepared technology, and poor delivery.

These monsters present their own unique challenges and choose their own prey. For some of you, Technology will present a minimal challenge, and you'll cage that monster quickly with more than enough skill to lock it back up if it ever pops up before or during your next webinar. For others, Technology will be your persistent nemesis—you'll fear and find it everywhere and lose to it at least once or twice.

The monsters called Content and Delivery are almost fraternal twins. They are, in many ways, very similar—they both have something to do with what's going to be covered, said, and discussed. But they're not quite identical in that one has to do with "what" will be covered and the other focuses on the "how." For some of us, getting the "what " clear and ready is not nearly as threatening as "how" we cover it. Some people can create it and others can communicate it.

127

Whatever the fear order, the key to caging the monsters is simple: get them in their cages early and keep them there until the final sign-off screen has run its course. The secret to getting them in their cages quickly is to know how each monster appears and to create a checklist to catch them early, lock them up, and focus on creating a quality webinar experience.

Sometimes the monsters, or at least elements of them, can be caged well in advance of your webinar. Sometimes you'll be fighting them right up to and even during the webinar. What follows are caging techniques you can implement as you prepare for and deliver your webinar to minimize the appearance of, and the damage from, these three beastly heads.

CAGE THE CONTENT MONSTER

When it comes to the Content monster, there are elements you can cage and there are some you cannot. The following techniques represent elements you can control, but some Content monsters are more challenging to cage.

CONTENT OVERLOAD

You may have a Content monster that is made up of three or four or five days worth of live content that you need to cram into a two-hour webinar. This monster can be tamed, but you will need to be crafty in how you cage it. There are two approaches to caging this beast:

SNIP or SPLIT.

Snip: Take your content and prune it, condense it, abridge it, summarize it, and boil it down until you are left with only core principles, skills, and techniques. Snipping requires you to ditch all of the excess content, stories, and exercises. But do it you must.

Split: If you can't leave anything out, then chunk it up into separate webinar sessions. You'll end up keeping much more of the original content, and participants will simply attend multiple sessions.

In our experience, we've found that webinars should be between 90 minutes and 2 hours. Max! If you need to use the split method, be sure the individual sessions follow this same time frame, with at least an hour between each session.

CONTENT BLOCK

In some instances, your Content monster could actually be in the form of another person, like a subject-matter expert or a designer. You may not have any content to begin with because your subject-matter expert isn't delivering what she promised, or you may have the content ready, but your instructional designer cannot get to it yet. Since this monster resides in others, this is also not an easy one to cage. You will need patience, perseverance, and charm. Good luck.

CONTENT STINK

Your Content monster could simply be that you have boring content. Dreadfully boring. Subject matter that stinks. This may not be something you can change, especially if it's mandatory content like compliance or regulatory training. Some content must remain in its original stinky state due to law or other formal requirements, but there are elements you can cage.

We recently spent a day knee-deep in just such content as we worked with an organization that trained government entities on how to write and submit a specific type of contract— typically, a three-day live training workshop. Bored yet? Our role was to help them break up 20 hours of very dry and detailed content into several manageable webinars. While the content had absolutely no sex appeal and could not be modified in the least, we were still able to help them build a successful webinar experience.

How did we do it? We employed the principles we introduced in "Shut Down the Ugly," "Humanize the Screen," and "Captivate or Alienate."

So even though it was challenging, we were still able to cage this monster by making it the best webinar possible by applying lipstick, makeup, and fancy clothes to the pig (or Content monster) and then sending it to finishing school. It was still a monster, but with less stink.

Here's how *The Webinar Manifesto* has been crafted to help you cage the Content monster.

1. Connect or Die

The greatest tool you have to cage a Content monster is simply having relevant and engaging content. Get out of your cubicle! Abandon your content-development silo! Reach out to content experts who have critical insights to share. This will increase the quality and relevance of your webinar content. So interact with as many people and groups as you can in preparing your webinar— participants, sponsors, customers, experts.

2. Don't Default

Get your platform, your hardware, and your software working with you rather than against you. Be creative in how you choose to use the webinar platform to present your content. If, for example, the platform is weak on video sharing, don't attempt to present your content that way. Rather, find creative ways to use other tools more powerfully and more effectively.

3. Shut Down the Ugly

This is where your primary weapons arsenal exists for caging and defeating Content monsters. Your ability to move from presenting and paralyzing to engaging and exciting will give your content optimal chance for success.

4. Captivate or Alienate

Virtual-accountability principles don't create content, but they do make it more user-friendly. Additionally, they help participants engage and remain engaged, especially at times or with certain parts of the webinar that particular participants may not initially be that engaged with.

5. Humanize the Screen

Your content means nothing if it dies on your side of the screen. Great content still needs to be pushed into your audience in engaging ways. Communication is a process, not just an idea. Pair quality content with good communication principles and your content will connect.

6. Crack the Feedback Code

Look at, listen to, and observe the visible and invisible feedback your audience gives you pertaining to your content. But don't stop there. Take this new information, modify your content, and throw it out there again. Rinse and repeat.

CAGING THE TECHNOLOGY MONSTER

Just like Typhon, the Technology monster has a hundred dragon heads, creating a multitude of threats, each with the potential to destroy your webinar.

131

THESE BEASTS LURK EVERYWHERE.

Unlike Content and Delivery, they're hard to clearly identify and flag. They pop up anyplace or anytime. Unpredictable.

Most of us have been bitten by the Technology monster at least once in our past. There was a time our webinar technology crashed on the very morning a critical client webinar was about to begin. No warning bells. No flashing lights. Just very angry clients who demanded our heads.

Yes, there have been times when an Internet connection went down. Or a phone line went bad. Most of us have experienced those moments of panic when, for some inexplicable reason, participants couldn't log into the session. Or when our key message, in the form of a large video file, froze, laying waste to all of our preparation.

Although there is no way to completely protect yourself, there are preventative steps you can take to ensure you are prepared for battle.

Technology Monster Prevention

LEVEL OF DIFFICULTY	POTENTIAL PROBLEM	PREVENTION PLAN
XX	Internet connection goes down.	Have two connections from different suppliers or a separate "air card" service through a cellphone provider.
XX	Telephone connection goes down.	Have a cell phone ready.
XX	Your computer dies.	Have a backup laptop or a copilot who can help drive the technology while you teach.
XX	Participants can't log on.	Have a technical-support number for them to call.
X	Videos don't play.	Test them several times before the live session.
XXX	Webinar technology crashes.	Have a secondary webinar service available.
XXX	The power goes out.	Have a secondary office nearby that you can run to.

Because the Technology monster lives everywhere, moves constantly, and spends substantial time in the shadows, it's critical that at every stage of content and delivery, you constantly check in on technology support and limitations. If you're not an expert in this area, find one—a real expert, not the guy in the next cubicle who *says* he's an expert. This is a great chance to practice the first principle of *The Webinar Manifesto*: "Connect or Die." Make doubly, triply, quadruply sure that the amazing tricks your content and delivery want to perform won't freeze-frame at the critical moment you need them.

CAGING THE DELIVERY MONSTER

Delivery is the handshake between content and audience. A lot of content wants to reach out and connect with your webinar audience but never quite makes it. Once again, some of the principles in *The Webinar Manifesto* are especially adapted to fighting this particular monster.

133

1. Don't Default

Platforms can kill presentations and strangle great participation. Awareness, Attempting, Assimilating, and Authoring are the key elements of this manifesto principle. Understand platform basics and figure out how to stretch them and then mold them for your unique purpose. This is the foundation of great delivery.

2. Shut Down the Ugly

Sustaining interest, maintaining focus, and managing learner/participant capacity all contribute to a presentation that people get hooked on, stay hooked to, and walk away able to remember what hooked them in the first place.

If your group doesn't get hooked fast, they start to drift, and that drift can be lethal. If they love your presentation but can't remember what it offered, they can't make the changes in behavior the content was all about in the first place.

3. Captivate or Alienate

Virtual accountability meets me on my turf and then invites me to play—fully engaged with both the content and the delivery. Merely having people on the webinar is neither a measure of, nor a guarantee of, success. They have to really be there, and the best content is never going to make that happen—you have to deliver.

4. Humanize the Screen

You have the charge to reach through that screen and make the virtual experience feel like a human experience. Look at me. Talk to me. Listen to me. Let me think. Don't bombard me with a constant barrage of information. Instead, let's have a regular conversation.

THE MONSTER-CAGING CHECKLIST

To cage these three monsters, you need a tool you can use before and during your webinar: the Monster-Caging Checklist.

134

Monster-Caging Checklist

TIME FRAME	CONTENT MONSTER	DELIVERY MONSTER	TECHNOLOGY MONSTER
Two Weeks Out	☐ Review the content flow and all of the materials.	☐ Send out the invitations to the webinar. ☐ Practice teaching the webinar with other people if possible.	☐ Identify and test all technical components.
Day Of Webinar	☐ Have materials on hand.	☐ Eliminate all sources of noise or interruptions. ☐ Place a "Do Not Disturb" sign on your door. ☐ Warm up your voice and get energized.	☐ Double-check your network connection. ☐ Close down all other applications and programs on your computer.
30-60 Min. Before		☐ Close your door and forward your calls. ☐ Eat and drink something for energy. ☐ Visit the restroom.	☐ Boot your computer up and get online. ☐ Confirm network and telephone connection.
10-30 Min. Before	☐ Get your training guide ready. ☐ Double-check content is ready for delivery.	☐ Place your headset on.	☐ Log on to your webinar and display your welcome screen.

Monster-Caging Checklist (cont.)

TIME FRAME	CONTENT MONSTER	DELIVERY MONSTER	TECHNOLOGY MONSTER
10 Min. Before		☐ Dial in and start welcoming participants.	☐ Check participants' network connections and telephone connections.
Start of Webinar		☐ Go over the webinar dos and don'ts.	
End of Webinar	☐ Suggest the next training event. ☐ Use polls to get any additional information you may want.	☐ Give them your email address for further contact. ☐ Point out the available downloads one more time.	☐ Explain the feedback-and-evaluation process for the webinar.

THE LAST LAST WORD

There's no need to go commando and head out looking for these monsters in remote places. They're already lurking in your webinar world right now. And if you haven't found them yet,

THEY WILL FIND YOU.
GUARANTEED.

It's their mission to destroy your webinar. They'll rear back their ugly heads the moment you let your guard down and fail to prepare for them.

Content, Technology, and Delivery are the biggest beasts you have to deal with during your webinar. No matter how well you follow all of the other principles in this manifesto, if you fail to cage these monsters,

YOU FAIL.
PERIOD.

YOU want to succeed because you have a message to share.

Your **ATTENDEES** want you to succeed because they've committed their time to learning something new.

WE want you to succeed because you have the chance to help turn around an industry that is suffering from neglect, sloppiness, apathy, carelessness, poor quality, and widespread abuse.

Together, let's never ever design, deliver, or sell lousy webinars again!

PUTTING PRINCIPLE TO PRACTICE (KEY SUMMARY POINTS)

The three webinar monsters you must face are:

1. Content Monster. Some elements of this monster can be caged and controlled, while others cannot.

   a. Content Overload. This Content monster appears when you are trying to cram too much content into a shorter webinar. Instead of cramming, you can snip or split it. Snipping is to condense and summarize. Splitting means keeping all of the original content but chunking it into multiple webinar sessions.

137

b. `Content Block`. If your subject-matter expert is too busy or unwilling to work within your deadlines, you will be defeated by this Content monster. Good luck next time.

c. `Content Stink`. Sometimes content is just plain boring and there is nothing you can do about it. To remedy this, try applying best thinking from the other manifesto principles in the book.

2. `Technology Monster`. This beasts lurks everywhere on your platform. While you cannot completely protect yourself from this unpredictable monster, you can use the Technology Monster Prevention tool to help minimize the surprises. Also, seek out platform experts who can help you battle this monster via the "Connect or Die" principles.

3. `Delivery Monster`. Great content and design will sometimes die at the hands of this monster. If your presenter is not adequately prepared, this monster will eat them up. Look for ways to apply the other manifesto principles in the book to beat this monster.

MANIFESTO CHRONICLES

Ideas, solutions, and other cool resources

WEBINAR MANIFESTO SCORECARD

How many webinar attendees:

How many completed the feedback form:

Check all that apply:

EVERYTHING WORKED THE WAY IT WAS SUPPOSED TO. IF NOT, WHY NOT? (Refer to the Monster-Caging Checklist.)

1. ☐ My network connection worked.

2. ☐ My videos played.

3. ☐ My platform tools worked the way they were supposed to.

4. ☐ My audio worked.

5. VIRTUAL ACCOUNTABILITY

☐ I made it clear, up front, that learners were expected to contribute verbally, visually, and kinesthetically.

6. VERBAL ACCOUNTABILITY

☐ I encouraged verbal comments, answers, and feedback.

7. VISUAL ACCOUNTABILITY

☐ I used storytelling to paint vivid pictures and I shunned ugly presentations and materials from my webinar.

8. KINESTHETIC ACCOUNTABILITY

☐ I involved learners through movement by pushing platform tools, having them pull down information and materials, and providing offline opportunities for participants to practice what they learned.

9. HUMANIZING SKILL ONE—LOOK AT ME

- ☐ I created a positive virtual presence where participants felt like I was actually looking at them.

10. HUMANIZING SKILL TWO—TALK TO ME

- ☐ I created an online experience where participants felt like I was talking directly to them and that they were in a conversation.

11. HUMANIZING SKILL THREE—LISTEN TO ME

- ☐ I created an online experience where participants felt like they were heard.

12. HUMANIZING SKILL FOUR—LET ME THINK

- ☐ I created an online experience that allowed participants enough time to think.

141

MY SCORE: Out of 12

ACTION: Pick one to three areas you can improve and get to work!

THE ATTENDEE PLEDGE

You may have many responsibilities including designing, delivering, and attending the occasional webinar. Or you may just be someone who attends webinars to learn or experience something new. In any case,

YOU NEED TO PLEDGE TO NEVER ATTEND A LOUSY WEBINAR EVER AGAIN.

You wield more POWER than you may realize. You are the end user, the learner, the buyer, the reason the rest of us webinar geeks design and deliver webinars in the first place.

Without you, we have no market—we are nothing but a strange crew of self-indulgent nerds. So if you don't like your webinar experience, tell us about it, or we'll keep believing you're happy with what you're experiencing. At the same time, we'll keep believing that bald is the new beautiful. And we'll continue to spread, and you'll continue to get lousy webinars.

Stop trying to not hurt our feelings by being kind and gentle on webinar feedback. Speak up! Your voice is, after all, the most important voice.

Now that you've read our book, you know what this manifesto represents. Make a stand. Tell us what you like and what needs fixing—now. Send your webinar designers and presenters a copy of *The Webinar Manifesto* or introduce them to theWebinarManifesto.com.

Remember, the next time you attend a poorly run webinar, you have the tools, in *The Webinar Manifesto*, to change that experience for yourself, the presenter, and everyone else. It will take courage, but we promise that the next webinar, rooted in the principles of *The Webinar Manifesto*, will be better—much better.

I (STATE YOUR NAME) PLEDGE TO:

Be a connector and share *The Webinar Manifesto* with those who need it.
Be an active webinar participant.
Give feedback openly and willingly.
Actively promote and support webinars that follow *The Webinar Manifesto* principles.

143

KUDOS

Thanks to all our friends and FranklinCovey family members for bringing this book to fruition. We thank Bob Whitman, Sean Covey, Shawn Moon, Scott Miller, Roger Godfrey, Adam Merrill, Dean Collinwood, Sam Bracken, Annie Oswald, Breck England, Terry Lyon, Pam Parkin, Michael Bettin, Harry Nelson, Courtney Mattson, Brad Augustin, Tyler Staten, Parker Donat, Zach Kristensen, Jody Karr, Matt Ashcraft, Cate Williams, Cassidy Back, Heather Ackley, Kelly Thompson, Guillaume Privat, Elliott Masie, Deb Lund, and the hundreds of thousands of webinar attendees and our many webinar facilitators.

Extra special thanks to our families for putting up with us as we wrote this book: Laura, Will, Emma, Josh, and Caroline (the Murdochs); and Soni, Chloe, Layla, Ruby, Gemma, and TJ (the Mullers).

ABOUT THE AUTHORS

FROM MATT

It was 1981; I was in the sixth grade and growing up in the western United States. I was one of only three students from my school selected to learn how to use a personal computer. We had only one. It looked like a large beige typewriter wired to a television set. It sat in the back of the classroom and we all looked at it with curiosity and suspicion. It was an Atari 800 and had 64K of RAM. It was considered a powerhouse by personal-computer standards at the time. But what I didn't know then is that the concept of this one device would change the world forever.

By the time I was 13 years old, my parents bought me something nobody else in the neighborhood had—my very own computer. Friends and neighbors came over to see this novelty. By this time, I was a skilled programmer and had learned how to create games, simple applications, and calculators that enabled me to complete my math homework. It was the forefront of the PC Revolution and I was riding the wave that was getting larger and faster. One day I vividly remember my best friend, who owned an Apple IIe, telling me that some day we would have a gigabyte of memory in our computers. At the time, I couldn't even fathom that concept—today you can purchase a portable external hard drive with terabyte of memory. I'm sure in three years, my *phone* will have a terabyte in it.

Since the sixth grade, I have owned more computers and computer devices than I can remember. I have evolved from saving my work on a cassette tape to floppy discs to hard drives to cloud computing—where this book is being written and saved. In the early 1980s, I would use my 300-baud modem to connect to Bulletin Board Systems (BBS)—the precursor to the Internet—where I would read information shared by other BBS users. It was a simple place to learn about new computer gadgets and programming techniques. It was the beginning of a revolution.

I now have multiple learning devices at home, and I'm connected through most of the relevant social-networking tools available today. I can't wait to learn what evolutionary path technology is going to take next.

Today I hold an M.B.A. from the University of Utah and spend my days as FranklinCovey's Global Director of Online Learning. This leaves my nights and weekends open for my wife, four children, and a dog.

FROM TREION

Let me start by sharing one very important—and relevant—demographic about myself. I was born, raised, and schooled in South Africa in the '70s and '80s. This is significant to note because the digital revolution didn't make it to the African continent until the late '80s/early '90s, which may explain why I didn't even get to turn on a computer for the first time until 1995. I was in my first quarter of college when I received an assignment to write a paper... on a computer. I still remember very clearly going to my English 101 teacher and asking if I could submit a handwritten paper instead. After listening to my very well-presented argument, he thought for a second and said no.

I nervously made my way over to the computer lab, where I actually sat at my computer for an hour before I had enough courage to ask the computer lab technician how to turn it on. With a little assistance from him, I not only learned how to turn it on, but also how to find the word processor. Then I looked down at the "QWERTY" keyboard—my new pen—and realized I was in real trouble. At that very moment, I had one of the biggest choices of my entire life to make: adapt or die. I was already far from home, surrounded by loud but nice people with great accents, and faced with so many new and wonderful options. Did I really have to learn how to use a computer?

I chose to adapt. But it took me a long time. That night it took me about 4 hours to write just one page. The next day it took me about 3½ hours to write the second page. Slowly but surely I not only became comfortable with the computer, but proficient with it. I do suffer from one major side effect that came from my late adoption though—I have never learned how to type properly. Instead of elegantly caressing the keys like most people, I end up stabbing at the keys with only a few fingers. Unorthodox? Yes. But despite this obvious disability, I am able to type quite quickly. It's not pretty though. In fact, most people who see me type have to leave the room because it distresses them so much.

The interesting part of this story is that it occurred just 15 years ago. Now I spend most of my days working and writing on a computer.

Being a late adopter only applies to the computer. Since then, I was one of the first PalmPilot users. I am one of those "crazies" who stood in line for an iPhone. I have written much of this book on the iPad. I am an active Facebook and Yammer user, blogger, and tweeter. My daily routine includes receiving and reading industry news via email, blogs, websites, and mobile phone applications. Even though it has only been 15 years since I started this evolutionary journey, I feel like I am keeping up with the pack.

Today I hold a master's degree in instructional design from Utah State University and am FranklinCovey's Chief eLearning Architect, responsible for developing all online-learning initiatives.

I've lived in Utah for the past 15 years, where I spend most of my "offline" time with my talented wife and five amazing children.

DO YOU WANT TO SEE *THE WEBINAR MANIFESTO* PRINCIPLES IN ACTION?

Now you can experience the world-renowned benefits of FranklinCovey training, no matter where you live or work around the globe, through world-class webinars.

Rooted in the principles found in *The Webinar Manifesto*, LiveClicks webinars put the high-quality instruction of FranklinCovey's live classroom training into expertly designed virtual classrooms. LiveClicks webinar workshops are led by our certified instructors or yours. You will experience:

- Captivating design.
- High-quality instruction.
- Engaging and interactive exercises.
- Compelling content.
- Award-winning videos.

Our catalog of titles includes topics such as leadership, productivity, time management, project management, business skills, and personal effectiveness. Plus, we can build custom webinars that meet your specific needs.

To learn more about LiveClicks webinars or to experience one for yourself, please visit www.franklincovey.com/liveclicks or call 888-576-1776.

ABOUT FRANKLINCOVEY

FranklinCovey (NYSE: FC) is a global company specializing in performance improvement. We help organizations achieve results that require a change in human behavior. Clients include 90 percent of the Fortune 100, more than 75 percent of the Fortune 500, and thousands of small and mid-size businesses, as well as numerous government entities and educational institutions. FranklinCovey has 46 direct and licensee offices providing professional services in 147 countries.

Our expertise is in seven areas:

- Leadership
- Execution
- Productivity
- Trust
- Sales Performance
- Customer Loyalty
- Education

For more information, go to www.franklincovey.com/tc.

RESOURCE SITES

TWITTER

Twitter can be an effective learning tool. We use it as a means of discovering and sharing learning fragments.
twitter.com/learningexplosn

BLOG

Read our blog posts as we look at the future of learning, interesting trends, and relevant learning news.
thelearningexplosion.com

BOOK WEBSITE

Access some of the tools we shared in this book and sign the manifesto at thewebinarmanifesto.com.

FACEBOOK

If Facebook is your social-media preference, then like us at facebook.com/thewebinarmanifesto.

LINKEDIN

To engage Matt and Treion in conversation, please connect with us directly on LinkedIn.com.
linkedin.com/in/mattmurdoch
linkedin.com/in/treionmuller

FREE STUFF

Go to thewebinarmanifesto.com and download a poster as well as two chapters from the audio version of our first book, *The Learning eXPLOSION: 9 Rules to Ignite Your Virtual Classrooms*.